Recruiting and Retaining America's Finest

Evidence-Based Lessons for Police Workforce Planning

Jeremy M. Wilson, Bernard D. Rostker, Cha-Chi Fan

Supported by the National Institute of Justice

Center on Quality Policing

A RAND INFRASTRUCTURE, SAFETY, AND ENVIRONMENT CENTER

This project was supported by grant number 2006-DD-BX-0025 awarded by the National Institute of Justice, U.S. Department of Justice. The opinions, findings, and conclusions or recommendations contained herein are those of the authors and do not necessarily represent the official position of the U.S. Department of Justice. This research was conducted under the auspices of the RAND Center on Quality Policing within the Safety and Justice Program of RAND Infrastructure, Safety, and Environment (ISE).

Library of Congress Cataloging-in-Publication Data

Wilson, Jeremy M., 1974-
  Recruiting and retaining America's finest : evidence-based lessons for police workforce planning / Jeremy M. Wilson, Bernard D. Rostker, Cha-Chi Fan.
    p. cm.
  Includes bibliographical references.
  ISBN 978-0-8330-5068-7 (pbk. : alk. paper)
    1. Police—Recruiting—United States. 2. Police—United States—Personnel management. I. Rostker, Bernard. II. Fan, Cha-Chi. III. Title.

  HV8141.W554 2010
  363.2'2—dc22

                                                        2010037247

Published 2010 by the RAND Corporation
1776 Main Street, P.O. Box 2138, Santa Monica, CA 90407-2138
1200 South Hayes Street, Arlington, VA 22202-5050
4570 Fifth Avenue, Suite 600, Pittsburgh, PA 15213-2665
RAND URL: http://www.rand.org/
To order RAND documents or to obtain additional information, contact
Distribution Services: Telephone: (310) 451-7002;
Fax: (310) 451-6915; Email: order@rand.org

Preface

A critical but oft neglected function of police organizations is management of the sworn officer force. While there is much attention to recruiting and retention, these are just tools for moving and maintaining career profiles that meet the needs and aspirations of officers and provide the rank/experience profiles desired by police departments. Police decisionmakers have little ability to assess their organization and environment to develop their own evidence-based personnel planning. Likewise, they receive little empirical guidance on how best to build and maintain their workforce. To help them, the National Institute of Justice supported RAND in conducting a national survey of large police agencies on their practices in recruitment, retention, and developing a data-driven workforce profile. We used the data obtained from this survey, combined with information on each community from the U.S. Census Bureau, the Bureau of Labor Statistics, and the FBI Uniform Crime Reports, to build models that explore these areas. Many of the lessons provided may be applicable to other agencies, large and small. More generally, this report should be of interest to policymakers and researchers concerned with understanding and responding to police personnel challenges.

This report builds on extensive RAND research in police recruitment and retention, including

- *Police Recruitment and Retention for the New Millennium: The State of Knowledge*, by Jeremy M. Wilson, Erin Dalton, Charles Scheer, and Clifford A. Grammich, Santa Monica, Calif.: RAND Corporation, MG-959-DOJ, forthcoming.

- *Police Recruitment and Retention in the Contemporary Urban Environment: A National Discussion of Personnel Experiences and Promising Practices from the Front Lines,* by Jeremy M. Wilson and Clifford A. Grammich, Santa Monica, Calif.: RAND Corporation, CF-261-DOJ, 2009.

- *To Protect and to Serve: Enhancing the Efficiency of LAPD Recruiting,* by Nelson Lim, Carl Matthies, Greg Ridgeway, and Brian Gifford, Santa Monica, Calif.: RAND Corporation, MG-881-RMPF, 2009.

- *Strategies for Improving Officer Recruitment in the San Diego Police Department,* by Greg Ridgeway, Nelson Lim, Brian Gifford, Christopher Koper, Carl Matthies, Sara Hajiamiri, and Alexis Huynh, Santa Monica, Calif.: RAND Corporation, MG-724-SDPD, 2009.

- *Recruitment and Retention: Lessons for the New Orleans Police Department,* by Bernard D. Rostker, William M. Hix, and Jeremy M. Wilson, Santa Monica, Calif.: RAND Corporation, MG-585-RC, 2007.

- *Police Personnel Challenges After September 11: Anticipating Expanding Duties and a Changing Labor Pool,* by Barbara Raymond, Laura J. Hickman, Laura L. Miller, and Jennifer S. Wong, Santa Monica, Calif.: RAND Corporation, OP-154-RC, 2005.

- "Police Personnel Crisis Needs Federal Leadership," by Jeremy M. Wilson, *Washington Post,* May 23, 2006.

- *Community Policing and Crime: The Process and Impact of Problem-Solving in Oakland,* by Jeremy M. Wilson and Amy G. Cox, Santa Monica, Calif.: RAND Corporation, TR-635-BPA, 2008.

- *Community Policing and Violence Prevention in Oakland: Measure Y in Action,* by Jeremy M. Wilson, Amy G. Cox, Tommy L. Smith, Hans Bos, and Terry Fain, Santa Monica, Calif.: RAND Corporation, TR-546-BPA, 2007.

- *Police-Community Relations in Cincinnati,* by K. Jack Riley, Susan Turner, John MacDonald, Greg Ridgeway, Terry L. Schell, Jeremy M. Wilson, Travis L. Dixon, Terry Fain, Dionne Barnes-Proby, and Brent D. Fulton, Santa Monica, Calif.: RAND Corporation, TR-333-CC, 2005.

All this research and still more is accessible through the RAND Recruitment and Retention Clearinghouse: http://www.rand.org/ise/centers/quality_policing/cops/. Developed specifically for police practitioners, the clearinghouse promotes evidence-based personnel planning by making staffing information (e.g., promising practices guides, research reports, commentaries and interviews, news articles, websites, tools, data) readily available in an easy-to-use, searchable forum.

This research was conducted under the auspices of the RAND Center on Quality Policing within the Safety and Justice Program of RAND Infrastructure, Safety, and Environment (ISE). The Center conducts research and analysis to improve contemporary police practice and policy. The mission of ISE is to improve the development, operation, use, and protection of society's essential physical assets and natural resources and to enhance the related social assets of safety and security of individuals in transit and in their workplaces and communities. Safety and Justice Program research addresses occupational safety, transportation safety, food safety, and public safety—including violence, policing, corrections, substance abuse, and public integrity.

Questions or comments about this monograph should be sent to the lead author, Jeremy Wilson (jwilson@msu.edu). Information about the Safety and Justice Program is available online (http://www.rand.org/ise/safety), as is information about the Center on Quality Policing (http://cqp.rand.org). Inquiries about research projects should be sent to the following address:

Greg Ridgeway, Director
Safety and Justice Program
RAND Corporation
1776 Main St.
Santa Monica, CA 90407-2138
310-393-0411 x7734
sjdirector@rand.org

Contents

Preface iii
Figures ix
Tables xi
Summary xiii
Acknowledgments xxi
Abbreviations xxiii

CHAPTER ONE
Introduction 1
The Dynamic Staffing Challenge 2
Objective 8
Approach 9
Limitations 11
Organization of the Report 12

CHAPTER TWO
The Personnel Situation 13
Size of Agencies 13
Vacancies, Applicants, and Hires 14
Recruitment Strategies and Incentives 22
Recruitment Standards 25
Compensation 27
Promotion 30
Retirement 31
Current Workforce 32

Attrition 36
Budgets 38

CHAPTER THREE
Factors Affecting the Supply of Police Recruits 41
Why Recruits Join Police Departments: The Basic Model 42
   An Economic Model of Why Recruits Join Police Departments 42
   A Simple Mathematical Model of Why Recruits Join Police
      Departments. 44
   The Basic Econometric Model. 45
   Results for the Basic Econometric Model. 46
Impact of the Crime Rate on Police Recruiting 48
Police Department Efforts to Improve Recruiting 51
   Recruiters and Recruiting Budget 51
   Advertising. 52
   Recruiting Incentives 54
Recruiting by Gender and Race/Ethnicity. 55

CHAPTER FOUR
Career Management. 59
Modeling the Police Department 60

CHAPTER FIVE
Evidence-Based Lessons for Personnel Planning 67
Improving Personnel Planning 69
   What We Learned About Personnel Data Limitations. 70
   Developing an Infrastructure for Evidence-Based Personnel Planning . . 72

APPENDIXES
A. Police Recruitment and Retention Survey Procedures 75
B. Survey Instrument 81

References 105

Figures

1.1.   The Bucket Metaphor and the Demand for Police Officers 3
1.2.   Attrition Is Widening the Hole 4
1.3.   The Shrinking Supply Is Tightening the Faucet 6
1.4.   Expanding Duties Increase the Demand for Police Officers 7
2.1.   Frequency Distribution of Sworn Officer Rate................... 14
3.1.   Frequency Distribution of Potential Recruits Classified by
        Their Reservation Wage... 43
3.2.   Aggregate Police Supply Curve................................. 44
3.3.   Number of Full-Time Sworn Recruiters 51
3.4.   Prevalence of Common Advertising Used by Police
        Departments.. 52
4.1.   Average Years-of-Service Profile............................... 61
4.2.   "Healthy" and "Unhealthy" Distributions of Officers by
        Decade of Service.. 62
4.3.   Distribution of Officers by Decade of Service Among
        Agencies with Higher Proportions of Officers in the First
        Decade of Service.. 64
4.4.   Distribution of Officers by Decade of Service Among
        Agencies with Lower Proportions of Officers in the First
        Decade of Service.. 64

Tables

2.1. Police Recruiting Budget 15

2.2. Number of Sworn Officer Vacancies, Applicants, and Hires, 2006 and 2007 16

2.3. Sworn Officer Vacancies by Rank, 2007 17

2.4. Recruitment Investment Metrics, 2006 and 2007 18

2.5. Extent to Which Factors Created Difficulties in Filling Vacancies 19

2.6. Race and Sex of Sworn Officer Applicants, 2006 and 2007 20

2.7. Race and Sex of Sworn Officers Hired, 2006 and 2007 20

2.8. Educational Level of Sworn Officers Hired, 2006 and 2007 20

2.9. Sworn Officers Hired with Civilian Law Enforcement and Military Experience, 2006 and 2007 21

2.10. Sworn Officers Who Completed the Academy and Probation, 2006 and 2007 21

2.11. Recruiting Methods Used by Police Agencies 22

2.12. Groups Targeted for Recruitment by Police Agencies 23

2.13. Recruitment Incentives Used by Police Agencies 24

2.14. Minimum Education Requirement for Officer Positions 25

2.15. General Requirements for Officer Positions 26

2.16. Reasons Preventing an Offer of Employment as an Officer ... 26

2.17. Base Annual Pay by Rank, 2007 28

2.18. Total Pay Compensation by Rank, 2007 29

2.19. Changes in Recruit Compensation and the Ability to Meet Recruitment Goals, 2006 30

2.20. Methods that Determine the Frequency of Promotional Exams 31

2.21.   Types of Agency Retirement Systems 32
2.22.   Attributes of Agency Retirement Plans............................32
2.23.   Authorized and Actual Strength by Position Type, 2006
        and 2007..33
2.24.   Distribution of Sworn Workforce by Race/Ethnicity and
        Sex, 2006 and 2007 34
2.25.   Distribution of Sworn Workforce by Rank and Years of
        Service, 2007..35
2.26.   Distribution of Sworn Officer Attrition by Rank, 2007 37
2.27.   Distribution of Sworn Officer Attrition by Years of Service,
        2007 38
3.1.   Econometric Results for Basic Model of Police Applicants..... 47
3.2.   Crime Rate Correlation Matrix 49
3.3.   Econometric Results for Basic Model of Police Recruits
        with Crime Rates Included 50
3.4.   Econometric Results for Basic Model of Police Recruits
        with Select Means of Advertising 53
3.5.   Econometric Results for Basic Model of Police Recruits and
        Gender-Specific Models.. 56
3.6.   Econometric Results for Basic Model of Police Recruits and
        Race-Specific Models..57
A.1.   Comparison of Respondents to the Target Population......... 77
A.2.   Survey Nonresponse by Substantive Section 78

Summary

A critical but oft neglected function of police organizations is personnel management. While much attention is given to recruiting and retention, these are only tools for accomplishing a larger, more important, and less discussed goal: achieving and maintaining the profile of officers by experience and rank that satisfies agency needs and officer career aspirations. Police agencies often have little ability to assess their organization and environment, and they receive little guidance on how best to build and maintain their workforces.

In this work, we sought to fill the gap of information on practices available to police agencies through a survey of police agencies on their recruitment and retention practices and how they can affect the profile of officers at differing ranks of service. The survey, sent to every U.S. police agency with at least 300 sworn officers, sought to document such characteristics as authorized and actual strength by rank, officer work and qualifications, compensation, and recruiting efforts. We used these data to provide an overview of current recruitment and retention practices, how they affected police personnel profiles, and to identify future research needs.

Agency Characteristics

We sent the survey to 146 agencies; 107 responded, yielding a 73-percent response rate. We limited the survey to agencies of at least 300 officers because we sought lessons on the largest personnel systems where cohort or year-group management comes into play. Unfortunately, many agencies failed to provide complete information. Response rates regarding questions on recruiting costs, attrition, and some departmental statistics were substantially lower. For many of these questions, we received responses from less than half the 146 we sought to survey.

Most of the agencies in our survey had 300 to 1,000 sworn officers, while a handful had more than 4,000. Nearly half had fewer than two officers per 1,000 residents, but nearly one in four had three or more per 1,000 residents.

Most of the responding agencies had a formal recruiting goal based on filling vacancies or hiring a specific number of officers by attribute, such as race/ethnicity, sex, education, or prior experience. Collective bargaining and hiring restrictions may influence how vacancies are filled. Nearly three in four surveyed agencies had a collective bargaining agreement, and one in ten had a legal hiring restriction, such as a consent decree or court order.

Reported recruiting budgets varied widely, from $0 to $2.2 million in 2007, with a mean of $67,491 and a median of $9,500. The mean recruiting budget in 2007 was about 40 percent higher than that in 2006. The proportion of agencies with a recruiting budget also increased from 58 percent in 2006 to 63 percent in 2007.

Most of the vacancies these agencies sought to fill were, not surprisingly, at the rank of officer. Nevertheless, on average, these agencies also sought to fill about ten vacancies per year in ranks above officer through captain.

The greatest difficulty agencies reported in filling vacancies was a lack of qualified applicants; nearly four in five agencies cited this as causing "some" or "much" difficulty for them. Time between application and employment offer was also cited as a difficulty by two in three agencies.

Most applicants, and hires, were white males; white males were even more represented among hires than they were among applicants. White females constituted about one in ten applicants and hires, while males and females of other races constituted smaller proportions of applicants than hires.

Nearly all agencies reported an educational requirement, typically high-school graduation. Other typical requirements included

- psychological testing (99 percent)
- medical test (99 percent)
- driver's license (98 percent)
- U.S. citizenship (97 percent)
- vision testing (93 percent)
- physical agility testing (91 percent).

Agencies also reported disqualifying candidates for a wide variety of reasons. Among the most common disqualifications were

- felony conviction (93 percent)
- suspended driver's license (93 percent)
- serious misdemeanor conviction (81 percent)
- excessive points on driving record (79 percent).

On average, more than one in three new hires had prior military experience, and one in five had prior law enforcement experience. More than two in five responding agencies reported giving credit toward seniority, compensation, or retirement for prior civilian law enforcement experience, and nearly one in three did so for military experience.

Not all hired eventually "hit the street." Some do not complete the academy or their probationary period. In 2007, agencies providing such information indicated that, on average, 87 percent of candidates completed the academy and, of those hired, 83 percent completed probation. On average, it took about 1.33 hires to put one officer "on the street" in 2006 and 2.23 hires to do so in 2007.

Agencies used a wide variety of recruiting methods. Among the most popular were

- career fairs (94 percent)
- Internet (89 percent)
- newspapers (81 percent)
- community organizations (79 percent)
- college outreach (75 percent)
- walk-in office (71 percent).

Most agencies reported targeting specific groups in their recruitment, including

- racial/ethnic minorities (80 percent)
- women (74 percent)
- college graduates (67 percent)
- military veterans (65 percent)
- candidates with prior police experience (53 percent)
- foreign-language speakers (50 percent).

Only 12 percent of agencies claimed not to recruit for any specific group.

Nearly every agency reported using some form of incentive in recruitment. Among the most popular were

- uniform allowance (95 percent)
- training salary (82 percent)
- reimbursement for college courses (73 percent)
- pay rate by assignment (62 percent)
- salary increase for college degree (56 percent).

Most agencies reported raising compensation to improve recruiting. Only one in three said increased compensation made recruitment easier, but, as noted below, increased compensation is among the strongest statistical predictors of recruitment success. On average, agencies are about five percent below their authorized number of officers and ten percent below their authorized level of civilian personnel. Attrition in a given year is most common among the most junior personnel, who may still be exploring career possibilities, and the most senior personnel, who are entering retirement.

How Agencies Attract Recruits

To determine what attracts recruits to an agency, be it adventurous or nonroutine work or a desire or opportunity to help make a community safer, we constructed multivariate models accounting for labor-market characteristics, "taste" for police work, and recruiting tools and incentives.

When controlling for number of police vacancies, city size, local labor-market conditions, police compensation, and compensation for other jobs, we found that only police compensation and city size had statistically significant effects on police recruiting. The likely appeal of compensation is obvious; we suggest city size is a proxy for the absolute number of candidates and variety of police work likely to be available.

Controlling for the above labor-market conditions plus crime rates showed crime rates also to have a positive effect on an agency's ability to recruit candidates. We suggest that areas with higher crime rates may have more appeal to candidates with a "taste" for police work by providing more adventurous or nonroutine work opportunities or chances to make a difference in a community.

Controlling for labor-market conditions and recruitment advertising, we found little effect of advertising on the number of recruits. While police compensation and city size had positive effects on numbers of recruits in this model, the only statistically significant advertising effect was for television. While agencies offer a wide variety of recruiting incentives, we found none to have a statistically significant effect on recruiting. The results suggest that less emphasis on advertising and more emphasis on reaching out to and compensating targeted candidates may prove most beneficial to recruiting.

We also constructed separate statistical models of recruiting for men, women, whites, and nonwhites. The results of these were generally consistent with our overall model: Compensation matters most in attracting recruits.

Career Management Issues

We used the results of our survey to identify career management issues that departments may be facing. Specifically, we identified agencies with more junior and more senior personnel than the sample average. On average, 48 percent of officers are in their first decade of service, 36 percent are in their second decade of service, and 17 percent are in their third decade of service (rounding accounts for the sum of 101 percent). Departments that do not meet a typical profile are likely to move between "boom" and "bust" as cohorts of differing size progress through the system. Once such oscillations begin, they are difficult to stop. In order to gain control of the system, departments facing such oscillations will need to change the normal attrition patterns or fill the year-of-service and experience voids by hiring experienced officers from other departments.

Departments with higher proportions of junior personnel than typical are likely to face two problems. First, they will have a dearth of personnel for training and supervisory positions. Second, given competition among large younger cohorts, personnel within them will have fewer prospects for promotion and may face corresponding career frustration. Most departments that had high proportions of officers in their first decade of service did so to compensate for a lack of officers in subsequent decades of service.

Departments with higher numbers of senior personnel will face their own problems. In the most extreme cases, as senior officers retire, less-experienced cohorts will not suffice to fill their ranks, and the average age of the force will decrease. This may be desirable, but if the size of the first-decade force is too small, it will not be able to sustain the desired year-of-service and grade standards.

Controlling attrition can be tricky and costly. Attrition among less-experienced officers who do not have a substantial stake in their department can be particularly difficult to control.

Future Research Needs

Unfortunately, limited information constrains the lessons we are able to draw from this survey. As noted, more than one in four agencies failed to respond to the survey. Many that did respond did not answer large numbers of questions. While we cannot identify every reason an agency failed to respond or answer a question, in providing technical assistance to those that did, we learn of several problems agencies have in collecting and maintaining data. These include limited access to data, scarcity of resources, and narrow data collection scope.

Regarding access to data, we learned not all data are electronically available. Data that are electronically available are often not available in a single database or in databases that can be easily aggregated. Personnel authorized to access the data are often outside police agencies and have other duties to fulfill.

Regarding scarcity of resources, it is not surprising that, given demands on staff, police agencies can have a difficult time collecting data, let alone collating and providing it for external purposes. Staff who can overcome the problems of limited data access have limited time, and there are limited financial resources for technical innovations to overcome them.

Regarding lack of data collection, some departments do not collect specific personnel information about their staff and organization. Why they do not do so is not clear.

Several local and national efforts can help overcome these problems. Chief among these would be leadership and support for ongoing national data collection, facilitating comparative and longitudinal analyses of police staffing. While the expansion and increased frequency of administrative surveys would help, the best data would be comprehensive (such as via master personnel files as opposed to surveys) and gathered in real time. This could be incorporated as part of a National Police Personnel Data Center. Because data without analysis are of little value, support for local and national analysis would also be necessary to derive lessons for the law enforcement community. Analysis could focus on assessing if, when, how, and under what circumstances recruitment and retention strategies work, the career and personal needs of officers are met, and the administrative goals of management are accomplished.

Acknowledgments

We owe many thanks for contributions made to the development of this monograph. We thank Senator Arlen Spector and the National Institute of Justice (NIJ) for supporting this work, and Brett Chapman for working with the project team as he coordinated this project on behalf of NIJ. Of course, there would be no results to share if it weren't for the many police practitioners and others who invested significant time in helping us to refine our survey instrument and in compiling and providing the data it requested. Many also shared valuable feedback along the way. We would like to thank those who provided specific statistical consultation, including Jim Hosek, Jacob Klerman, and Greg Ridgeway, as well as Melanie Sisson and Terry Fain, who helped to compile and transform various portions of the data. Additionally, RAND' Survey Research Group administered the survey. Several others helped to improve the quality of the final monograph, including Edward Maguire and Lois Davis and NIJ's peer reviewers, who provided substantive comments on the draft, and RAND's editorial and publication staff.

Abbreviations

COPS Office   U.S. Department of Justice, Office of Community Oriented Policing Services

NDLEA   National Directory of Law Enforcement Administrators

CHAPTER ONE

Introduction

A critical but oft neglected function of police organizations is management of the sworn officer force. While there is much attention to recruiting and retention, these are just tools for moving and maintaining career profiles that meet the needs and aspirations of officers and provide the rank/experience profiles desired by police departments. Police decisionmakers have little ability to assess their organization and environment to develop their own evidence-based personnel planning lessons. Likewise, they receive little empirical guidance on how best to build and maintain their workforce.

Recent economic difficulties have catapulted the issue of police staffing into the forefront of national discussion. The COPS Hiring Program, with $1 billion in congressional funding to help stabilize law enforcement positions, received requests totaling $8.3 billion to support more than 39,000 sworn officer positions (COPS Office, 2009). Those familiar with police staffing contend that larger systemic trends continue to make it challenging to staff police organizations with qualified, diverse, and effective personnel.

Some may contend that recent recessionary times, and resulting high unemployment, have solved the staffing problem by overrunning agencies with applications. But the problem is not so simple. First, the systemic issues and trends, including those in qualifications, generational preferences, and attrition, affecting police recruitment and retention transcend economic conditions—and are likely to be exacerbated when economic conditions improve. Second, agencies overwhelmed by applications must still determine which and how many applicants to recruit—that is, they must still determine which are the best qualified and most committed to law enforcement as a career. Third, some agencies report continuing decreases in applications and particular difficulty in recruiting and maintaining a workforce that reflects their community. Fourth, agencies must still determine the career profile that best meets their needs, using recruitment and retention as the tools to ensure a proper staffing distribution. Fifth, police decisionmakers typically have little time, resources, and expertise for developing their own data-driven lessons on personnel planning, and researchers have provided them few lessons on what works. Information on promising practices tends to be anecdotal, entirely qualitative, limited in scope, or centered on the experience of a single person or agency (Switzer, 2006; Scrivner, 2006), thereby limiting the extent to which any particular agency can draw meaningful lessons for itself. All of this means that recruitment, retention, and career management will remain important challenges to police decisionmakers and communities.

The Dynamic Staffing Challenge

Police agencies face many challenges in filling their workforce needs. First, they must determine the experience and rank structure of their personnel that will most cost-effectively meet their needs. Second, they must select and use recruiting and retention tools that will foster their goals, taking into account such problems as the retirement of older cohorts, changing work preferences of younger generations, and decreasing funds for a steady or even expanding scope of work.

Wilson et al. (forthcoming) uses the metaphor of a bucket to illustrate some of the problems in managing departments with an ever-changing workforce environment. In this metaphor, the size of the bucket represents the absolute demand for police officers regardless of internal personnel structure and allocation. Water inside the bucket reflects the current level of police strength able to fulfill the demand. The size of the demand "bucket" or the amount of staffing "water" to fill are being affected in three ways: The hole draining the bucket of current staffing is widening, the faucet replenishing staff is tightening, and the width of the bucket representing the scope of police work is widening.

Even in the best circumstances, police agencies often find that they cannot fill the bucket. The current level of staffing is nearly always below the allocated level of staffing. Even the allocated level may not be enough to fulfill unmet demand (Figure 1.1).

The current level of staffing is being drained by a widening hole with several causes (Figure 1.2). These include

- *"Baby-boom" generation retirements.* In Chicago, for example, an early retirement option is expected to increase from about 500 to nearly 900 the deficit of officers below the authorized level of 13,500—a problem exacerbated by the department's wait for federal funding for new academy classes (Spielman, 2009).
- *Changing career preferences of younger generations.* Lower salaries than are available in the private sector, competition from the military, negative public perceptions of law enforcement, lower levels of organizational commitment, and a lack of interest by younger Americans in policing may all be dampening interest in police work among those entering the work force (Jordan et al., 2009; Pomfret, 2006; Egan, 2005; Tulgan, 2000; Wheeler, 2008; Twenge and Campbell, 2008).

Figure 1.1
The Bucket Metaphor and the Demand for Police Officers

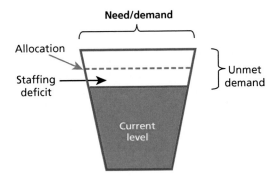

**Figure 1.2
Attrition Is Widening the Hole**

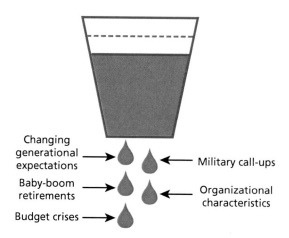

- *Military call-ups.* Many police officers serve in the military reserves. Increasing use of reserve forces in military operations overseas has depleted police forces at home. In the year ending June 30, 2003, 21 percent of local police departments had full-time personnel called to serve (Hickman and Reaves, 2006).
- *Budget constraints.* Two extreme cases of the effects decreasing financial support can have on police retention are evident in New Orleans and San Diego. New Orleans suffered particularly high losses from officers relocating to better-paying jurisdictions after Hurricane Katrina (Rostker, Hix, and Wilson, 2007; Wilson, Rostker, and Hix, 2008). In San Diego, uncompetitive wages and salary freezes led many officers to seek better opportunities elsewhere, including a detective with more than 20 years of experience who applied for a patrol position in a neighboring community (Manolatos, 2006).
- *Other organizational characteristics.* In addition to those noted above, officers may choose to leave a department for still other reasons, including the characteristics of their immediate supervisor, lack of career growth, unmet job expectations, inadequate

feedback, insufficient recognition, or lack of training (Orrick, 2008a, 2008b; Wilson and Grammich, 2009).

There appear to be five main influences on why officers may leave an agency: (1) the pull of other opportunities, (2) actual and potential compensation, (3) personal characteristics and demographic variables, (4) organizational health, policy, and culture, and (5) employee needs (Lynch and Tuckey, 2004). Police turnover can be problematic for several reasons. Police employee success is a function of experience and ability to make sensible decisions with minimal oversight (Frost, 2006; Gottfredson and Gottfredson, 1988). Reducing the number of officers with experience inhibits effective decisionmaking and diminishes department strength and cohesion. This is similar to problems other fields experience in "brain drain" following voluntary separations that reduce performance levels and increase operational risks (Birati and Tziner, 1995; Mobley, 1982; Holtom et al., 2008). Nevertheless, the cost of training sworn police officers is substantial in comparison to other fields (New South Wales Council on the Cost of Government, 1996), although levels of turnover for police appear to be lower than that for other occupations (Cooper and Ingram 2004). The high level of organizational and job-specific knowledge that police officers require means that high turnover can impair organizational performance.

The faucet of supply that can replenish the bucket is also tightening for several reasons (Figure 1.3). The militaristic nature of police work may be less likely to appeal to younger generations for many of the same cultural reasons that have reduced youth propensity to join the military (Bowyer, 2007; U.S. Department of Defense, 2003; Wilson, 2000). Altogether, fewer than half of U.S. youths consider a police agency a "desirable" or "acceptable" place to work (National Research Council, 2003). Increasing proportions of younger generations are unable to meet the qualifications for police work, including a clean criminal record, little to no drug use, physical fitness, and financial stability (see Johnston et al., 2008, on drug use; Sturm et al., 2004, on fitness; and Draut and Silva, 2004, as well as Draut, 2008, on debt). Police applicants today must have a wider range of skills than those of earlier years; educated workers meeting present standards for law

Figure 1.3
The Shrinking Supply Is Tightening the Faucet

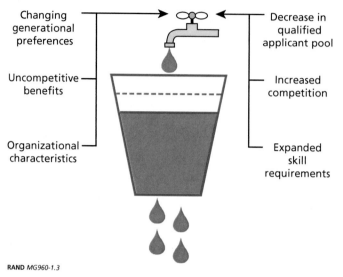

Changing generational preferences

Decrease in qualified applicant pool

Uncompetitive benefits

Increased competition

Organizational characteristics

Expanded skill requirements

RAND *MG960-1.3*

enforcement position have more job prospects, making it difficult to recruit them to the field. Other agencies, including the military and the growing homeland security industry, increasingly compete for those that are qualified (Kane, 2005; Frawley, 2006; DeRugy, 2006; Kondrasuk, 2004; and Makinen, 2002). Many potential applicants perceive the financial benefits of police work to be increasingly uncompetitive with those of similar or other work (for more on officer salaries and those in the private sector, see Hickman and Reaves, 2006, and U.S. Bureau of Labor Statistics, 2009). Organizational characteristics, such as the image of a particular agency, especially for minority candidates, can discourage the flow of applicants (Wilson and Grammich, 2009; Wright, 2009).

While the hole draining current staff is widening and the faucet replenishing staff is tightening, the bucket of demand is also widening as local police agencies are asked to undertake new, more complex tasks (Figure 1.4). In the past two decades, most police agencies have adopted some form of community policing (Maguire and Mastrofski, 2000; Wilson, 2006; Zhao, Lovrich, and Thurman, 1999). This has

Figure 1.4
Expanding Duties Increase the Demand for Police Officers

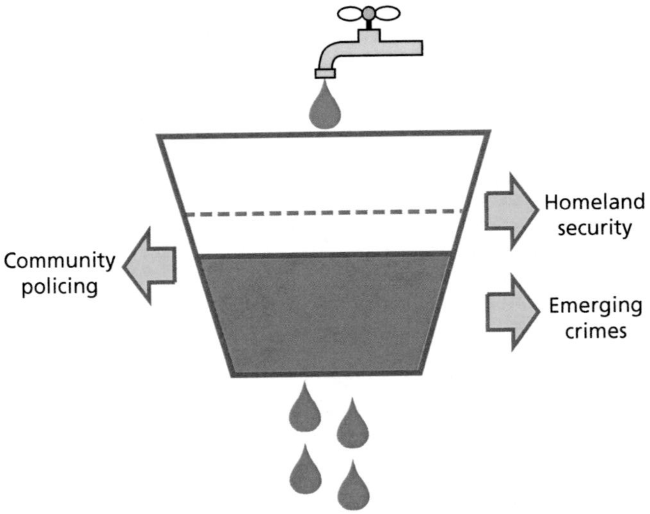

Community policing

Homeland security

Emerging crimes

RAND *MG960-1.4*

changed the nature of much traditional police work, requiring police to collaborate with local citizens in maintaining order in their communities (Hickman and Reaves, 2006). Homeland security demands have required local police to perform additional patrol and surveillance, gather and analyze counterterrorism intelligence, increasingly enforce immigration laws, and participate in various task forces that coordinate such work among multiple agencies. Globalization and technological advancement are contributing to a greater awareness of still other crimes, such as human trafficking, identity theft, and cybercrime, requiring the attention of local police.

Finally, economic changes affect the ability of police agencies to fill the bucket in many, sometimes contradictory ways. Recently increasing unemployment has caused some departments to be inundated with applications from workers who come from a variety of industries. Yet this increasing applicant pool raises concerns, including those about the ability of agencies to screen higher numbers of applicants and the continuing interest of these applicants in police work once conditions in other industries improve. Furthermore, the same economic conditions that are leading to increased unemployment are also adversely affecting the ability of police agencies to hire young, talented officers—the very officers departments will need in the future for its leadership.

Even when economic conditions improve, long-term systemic changes will likely continue to pose staffing problems for local police agencies. In particular, past hiring booms and freezes will create difficulties as they ripple through the organization over time, from field training to retention, and as police agencies determine how best to replenish officers leaving the force over time and to replace the benefits of their experience.

The bucket example illustrates the problem that police departments face in recruiting and retaining officers to meet the expanding demands. This is but part of their personnel management challenge. Most departments have not been able to "shape" the age and experience profiles of their personnel. As a result, they find themselves struggling to address such issues as having too many recruits, not having enough patrol officers to provide field training, or waves of retirement for experienced career officers. Distribution of personnel by years of service also affects career opportunities, promotion rates, retention, and total personnel costs for departments.

Objective

As we earlier noted, many departments do not have time to develop their own lessons learned for personnel recruitment, retention, and management. Research on relevant practices is also limited. The primary objective of this monograph is to formulate evidence-based lessons on recruitment, retention, and managing workforce profiles in large police departments. It extends the extant literature on personnel planning by focusing on empirical analysis and by placing recruitment and retention in a larger context of managing the police workforce and its structure.

Approach

To develop evidence-based lessons for personnel planning in large agencies, we sought to survey every U.S. municipal police agency with at least 300 sworn officers on their current personnel profiles and the effectiveness of their recruitment and retention programs. The sampling frame for our survey was the 2007 National Directory of Law Enforcement Administrators (NDLEA). The NDLEA is a standard, comprehensive list of police agencies that has been used as the sampling frame for national surveys in previous studies that have passed rigorous peer review (Jordan et al., 2009; Davis et al., 2006; Taylor et al., 2006; Riley et al., 2005; Davis et al., 2004; Gilmore Commission, 2003).

Through the survey and analysis of other variables (e.g., population size, unemployment rate) for each jurisdiction we surveyed, we sought to answer the following questions:

- What is the personnel situation that large agencies currently encounter? What approaches have they taken or what problems do they perceive in recruiting, compensating, promoting, and retaining personnel? How do these perceived problems vary by agency characteristics, such as size?
- What affects the supply of police recruits? What economic variables might affect how many perceived problems compare to likely actual ones? How might crime rates affect the number of recruits a police department can attract?
- What challenges might agencies face in career management? How does the profile of their officers by experience and rank compare to an ideal one that can avoid oscillations from very senior to very junior forces? What agencies do to control oscillations once they start?

We developed the instrument based on our experience in working with large personnel systems, instruments used in previous police staffing surveys (Taylor et al., 2006; U.S. Department of Justice, 2006; and Koper, Maguire, and Moore, 2002), and discussions with police practitioners. We then conducted two rounds of pretesting and refined the instrument based on feedback from the police departments in Columbus, Ohio; Las Vegas, Nevada; Dallas, Texas; New Orleans, Louisiana; and Pittsburgh, Pennsylvania.

We distributed the initial surveys on February 27, 2008. To ensure an acceptable response rate, we developed a comprehensive nonresponse protocol, provided ample field time for departments to compile information and respond, and provided significant one-on-one technical assistance to agencies as they completed the survey. In all, the surveys were in the field for 38 weeks.

From 146 departments with at least 300 sworn officers, we received 107 completed surveys (six departments refused, and the remainder provided no contact or information). This 73-percent response rate is favorable given the complexity of the survey. We supplemented this survey with data on each jurisdiction from the American Community Survey conducted by the U.S. Census Bureau, the Bureau of Labor Statistics, and the FBI Uniform Crime Reports.

We compared several characteristics of responding agencies with all agencies in our sample. Responding agencies were comparable to all agencies in the sample on all available measures: size of agency and community, region, annual wage earned in the community, unemployment, and violent and property crime.

Together, these are the sources of data on which we develop the models of recruitment, retention, and workforce profiles that illustrate empirical lessons. We tested all regression models for multicollinearity by calculating the variance inflation factors and for heteroscedasticity using White's general test (White, 1980). More detail on these tests and processes is provided in appropriate sections below. Given our relatively small sample, we chose 0.10 as our level of statistical significance, as others recommend for this type of policy research (Hayes and Daly, 2003; Lipsey, 1990; McGarrell and Hipple, 2007; Sherman and Strang, 2004; Sherman, Strang, and Woods, 2000). This permitted us to identify relationships that might exist at a lower alpha level had the sample had been larger, but, compared with the standard 0.05 level of significance, increases the likelihood of identifying relationships that truly do not exist in the population. To allow readers to make their own determinations, we indicate the alpha level (0.10, 0.05, 0.01) for all statistical tests.

We discuss our survey procedures and nonresponse analysis more thoroughly in Appendix A and present a copy of the survey questionnaire in Appendix B.

Limitations

As with any study, our analysis has a number of data limitations. Larger samples are typically preferable. While our response rate is fairly high, higher nonresponse to some items limits the ability of our models to detect statistical relationships and reduces the precision of our estimates.[1] Some data provided were internally inconsistent, thereby requiring us to make assumptions about how to use specific variables. While we gathered data on a number of strategies to bolster recruitment, we have little information on the form, substance, and dosage or amount of the strategy. For strategies not found to be statistically related to numbers of applications, the lack of implementation information prevents us from determining whether specific strategies are ineffective or were not used properly. We also do not know the extent to which changes in numbers of applicants correspond to changes in the quality of applicants or desired attributes. Finally, our sample is based on large municipal police organizations. While some of the lessons we provide may extend to smaller or other types of police organizations (e.g., county, state, tribal, federal), we cannot attest the extent to which they might. We highlight these and other limitations throughout the monograph.

---

[1]   We considered using imputation methods to address nonresponse, but most such techniques require an assumption that the data are missing at random (i.e., the probability that an observation is missing does not depend on its value, or the missing data values contain no information about the probabilities of being missing). We do not have enough evidence and intuition to support this assumption. Additionally, imputed data do not perfectly represent true values and therefore introduce "noise" that is difficult to evaluate.

Organization of the Report

In the next chapter, we describe the state of personnel characteristics and experiences in 2006 and 2007, or just before the time of our 2008 survey. We highlight the variation that exists even among the largest police organizations. In the third chapter, we explore statistical models for assessing the empirical relationships between organizational and community characteristics and the volume of applicants received by police organizations. In the fourth chapter, we detail the relationship of recruitment and retention with the distribution of the workforce by experience and the implications of this relationship for personnel planning and management. In the final chapter, we summarize promising lessons for improving personnel planning and note issues requiring further attention.

CHAPTER TWO

The Personnel Situation

In this chapter, we explore the characteristics and experiences of large police agencies in workforce planning and management. We summarize descriptive information for 2006 and 2007 as provided by the agencies responding to our survey. Each table provides the number of agencies on which the information is based. For many key variables and where nonresponse bias would most likely exist (variables with fewer respondents) we tested (by comparison of means tests) for systematic differences between those that responded and those in the target population. We examined differences in terms of several organizational and community characteristics: agency size, city size, region, annual community wage, unemployment rate, and violent and property crime rates. We footnote in the corresponding sections which variables we tested (the tests revealed no statistically significant differences for any of the variables). The substantive results illustrate that there is considerable variation even among this group of "large" agencies.

Size of Agencies

There is considerable variation by size and other characteristics among these "large" agencies. The number of agencies responding to the survey distributed by their number of sworn officers was

- 31 with 300 to 399
- 47 with 400 to 999
- 29 with 1,000 to 3,999
- 4 with at least 4,000.

The agencies also varied in their numbers of sworn officers per 1,000 residents. Nearly half had fewer than two officers per 1,000 residents, but nearly one in four had three or more per 1,000 residents (Figure 2.1).

Vacancies, Applicants, and Hires

Most of the agencies (77 percent) indicated that they had a formal hiring goal in 2006, based on filling vacancies or hiring a specified number of officers based on race/ethnicity, sex, education, prior police or military experience, or some other attribute. Collective bargaining and hiring restrictions may influence the way in which agencies fill these positions. Seventy-three percent of the surveyed agencies had a collective bargaining agreement, and 10 percent had a legal hiring restriction, such as a federal consent decree or court order.

Figure 2.1
Frequency Distribution of Sworn Officer Rate

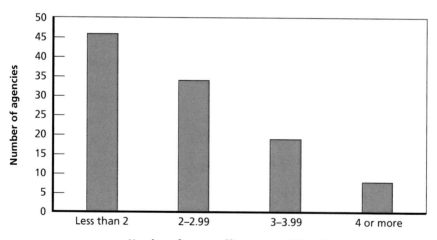

RAND MG960-2.1

Recruiting budgets (excluding personnel costs) and number of recruiters indicate the investment that agencies are making in filling their workforce needs and the flexibility they have to do so. Reported recruiting budgets ranged from $0 to $1.2M in 2006 and $0 to $2.2 million in 2007 (Table 2.1). The mean recruiting budget in 2007, $67,491, was about 40 percent higher than in 2006. The proportion of agencies with a recruiting budget also increased from 58 percent in 2006 to 63 percent in 2007. On average, all the agencies in our sample reported having nearly four sworn officers and one civilian assigned full time to the recruiting process. These findings must be interpreted cautiously. Recruiting for some agencies may be conducted by another organization (e.g., a city human resource bureau) or impossible to separate for budget and reporting purposes. This might lead to some agencies reporting a budget of $0 or having zero recruiters when in fact their cities have invested in police recruiting.

In 2007, the average agency received more than 2,200 applications for 73 vacancies (see Table 2.2).[1] Not surprisingly, vacancies were concentrated in the rank of officer, with a mean 55 vacancies (median of 24), but there was also a mean of five sergeant vacancies, two lieutenant vacancies, and one captain vacancy per department (Table 2.3). This translated into the average vacancy rates by rank being the same and highest for officer and captain at 13 percent. On average, agencies

Table 2.1
Police Recruiting Budget

Year	Minimum	Maximum	Median	Mean	Standard Deviation	n
2006	0	1,200,000	5,000	48,938	138,750	107
2007	0	2,200,000	9,500	67,491	232,005	107

[1]   We detected no statistically significant differences between agencies that reported applications for 2006 and 2007 and the target population.

Table 2.2
Number of Sworn Officer Vacancies, Applicants, and Hires, 2006 and 2007

	2006				2007			
	Median	Mean	Standard Deviation	n	Median	Mean	Standard Deviation	n
Total vacancies	—	—	—	—	35	73.25	125.18	99
Total applied	451	2,247	8,443	65	502	2,219	7,952	69
Total hired	40	98	325	90	48	99	263	91

hired 99 officers each in 2007.[2] The average number of applications and hires remained relatively stable from 2006 to 2007.

Based on these data, we gauged the "selectivity" of the agencies by calculating the number of applications each agency received per vacancy. Ranging from 0 to 218, on average 27 persons applied for each vacancy in 2007, with agencies receiving a mean 21 applications for each person hired.

In 2007, on average, agencies invested more than $1,500 in recruiting candidates for each vacancy; mean expenditures per vacancy ranged from $0 to $35,515 (Table 2.4). On average, agencies also spent just over $100 per applicant and $1,200 per hire, with the highest amount paid to fill each vacancy more than $35,000.

We asked respondents what might influence their organization's ability to fill vacancies and the extent to which they do so. Agencies reported having the most trouble in securing qualified applicants (i.e., those meeting the agency's minimum standards), with 29 percent saying it creates "much difficulty," and an additional 50 percent saying it creates "some difficulty" (Table 2.5). Of the factors listed, the benefits package provided by the agencies appears to be the least problematic in filling vacancies.

---

[2]   The difference between hires and vacancies is likely due to the different reporting time line of these metrics. "Hires" are based on the entire year, whereas "vacancies" are based on those recorded at the beginning of the year. Agencies likely hired to fill vacancies that came open throughout the year that were not counted (because they did not exist) at the beginning of the year.

Table 2.3
Sworn Officer Vacancies by Rank, 2007

Rank	Median	Mean	Standard Deviation	n	Mean Vacancy Rate by Rank	Standard Deviation	n	Mean Proportion of Total Vacancies	Standard Deviation	n
Highest ranking officer	0	0.07	0.25	107	0.07	0.26	68	0.02	0.12	92
Below highest ranking but above captain	0	0.46	1.16	107	0.09	0.20	70	0.02	0.07	92
Captain	0	1.11	3.99	107	0.13	0.35	67	0.02	0.05	92
Lieutenant	0	1.61	3.20	107	0.06	0.10	64	0.04	0.07	92
Sergeant	1	5.32	13.01	107	0.05	0.05	63	0.10	0.12	92
Below sergeant but above officer	0	3.86	15.96	107	0.08	0.16	31	0.05	0.11	92
Officer	24	55.36	109.60	107	0.13	0.26	64	0.75	0.25	92
Total	35	73.25	125.18	99	0.09	0.14	67	—	—	—

Table 2.4
Recruitment Investment Metrics, 2006 and 2007

	2006						2007					
	Minimum	Maximum	Median	Mean	Standard Deviation	n	Minimum	Maximum	Median	Mean	Standard Deviation	n
Recruit budget per vacancy	—	—	—	—	—	—	0	35,515	328	1,522	4,219	92
Recruit budget per applicant	0	45,518	27	821	5,820	61	0	1,144	25	113	232	67
Recruit budget per hire	0	45,518	198	1,297	5,141	86	0	35,515	323	1,206	3,924	89

NOTE: The 2006 metrics are influenced by one agency with a recruitment budget substantially higher than the average, which had only a small, and equal, number of applicants and hires. This agency did not provide data for 2007.

Table 2.5
Extent to Which Factors Created Difficulties in Filling Vacancies

Factors	No Difficulty	Some Difficulty	Much Difficulty	N/A	n
Lack of qualified applicants	18%	50%	29%	3%	107
Time between application and employment offer	29%	51%	16%	4%	107
Level of entry pay	52%	34%	8%	6%	106
Recruits failing to complete training	23%	65%	5%	7%	103
Image of officers/ department in community	67%	25%	3%	4%	106
Benefits package	69%	24%	2%	6%	106

Applications (Table 2.6) and hiring (Table 2.7) by race and sex appear to have been stable in 2006 and 2007 among agencies supplying such data to us. About half of the applicants were white males. About one-third were males of another race. White females and females of another race each constituted about one in ten applicants. Relative to applicants, white males represent a higher proportion of hires, and males and females of another race represent smaller proportions, but whether the hiring processes represent an adverse impact for any group is beyond the purpose and data of our study. Most hires had at least some college education (Table 2.8).

We asked whether agencies provided any credit, be it toward seniority, compensation, or retirement, for prior civilian law enforcement or military experience. Forty-one percent of the reporting agencies gave some kind of credit for civilian law enforcement experience; 32 percent gave credit for military experience (Table 2.9).[3] Sizable minorities of hires have these experiences, particularly military experience.

---

[3] We detected no statistically significant differences between agencies that reported hires with civilian or military experience in 2006 and 2007 and the target population.

Table 2.6
Race and Sex of Sworn Officer Applicants, 2006 and 2007

	2006			2007		
	Mean Proportion	Standard Deviation	n	Mean Proportion	Standard Deviation	n
White males	0.53	0.19	61	0.51	0.19	67
White females	0.10	0.08	61	0.10	0.07	67
Other males	0.29	0.17	61	0.30	0.18	67
Other females	0.08	0.08	61	0.09	0.09	67

Table 2.7
Race and Sex of Sworn Officers Hired, 2006 and 2007

	2006			2007		
	Mean Proportion	Standard Deviation	n	Mean Proportion	Standard Deviation	n
White males	0.61	0.18	86	0.60	0.19	89
White females	0.09	0.06	86	0.09	0.06	89
Other males	0.24	0.16	86	0.25	0.17	89
Other females	0.05	0.06	86	0.05	0.06	89

Table 2.8
Educational Level of Sworn Officers Hired, 2006 and 2007

	2006			2007		
	Mean Proportion	Standard Deviation	n	Mean Proportion	Standard Deviation	n
High school graduates	0.46	0.37	68	0.41	0.35	70
Some college	0.26	0.23	68	0.30	0.26	70
College graduates	0.28	0.26	68	0.29	0.25	70

Table 2.9
Sworn Officers Hired with Civilian Law Enforcement and Military Experience, 2006 and 2007

	2006			2007		
	Mean Proportion	Standard Deviation	n	Mean Proportion	Standard Deviation	n
Had prior civilian law enforcement experience	0.21	0.25	47	0.20	0.21	48
Had prior military experience	0.35	0.53	44	0.37	0.47	46

Of course, not all hired eventually "hit the street." Some do not complete the academy or are let go during their probationary period. In 2007, agencies providing such information indicated that, on average, 87 percent completed the academy and, of those hired, 83 percent completed probation (Table 2.10). By dividing the number of hires by the number of those completing probation for each agency (raw data not shown), we calculate that, on average, it took about 1.33 hires to put one officer "on the street" in 2006, and 2.23 hires in 2007.

Table 2.10
Sworn Officers Who Completed the Academy and Probation, 2006 and 2007

	2006			2007		
	Mean Proportion	Standard Deviation	n	Mean Proportion	Standard Deviation	n
Officers who completed the academy	0.92	0.28	83	0.87	0.26	84
Officers who completed probation	0.90	0.21	81	0.83	0.38	74

Recruitment Strategies and Incentives

There are many ways police agencies can share information about their organization, increase awareness of vacancies, and directly recruit applicants. Agencies in our survey report using numerous recruitment methods (Table 2.11). The most common forms of recruitment, used by more than 80 percent of agencies, are holding career fairs, marketing on the Internet, and advertising in newspapers. Among the least

Table 2.11
Recruiting Methods Used by Police Agencies

Recruiting Method (*n*=107)	Proportion
Career fairs	0.94
Internet	0.89
Newspapers	0.81
Community organizations	0.79
College outreach	0.75
Walk-in office	0.71
Posters	0.69
Military installations	0.65
Explorer/cadet program	0.63
Radio	0.61
High school outreach	0.52
College internships	0.52
Magazines	0.48
Television	0.45
Billboards	0.34
Mass mailings	0.32
Open house at police department	0.29
Other	0.28

common strategies were advertising on billboards, conducting mass mailings, and hosting open houses, though even these methods are used by about one in three agencies providing information on this question.

Most agencies report making specific efforts to recruit particular groups (Table 2.12). Four in five recruit specifically for minorities, and three in four recruit specifically for women. At least half also recruit for college graduates, military veterans, those with police experience, and foreign language speakers. Only 12 percent claimed to not recruit for any particular group. One in six agencies have enlisted the support of advertising agencies or professional marketing firms in crafting their recruitment campaign.

Nearly every agency used some form of incentive in recruitment (Table 2.13). Among the most common ones are a uniform allowance,[4] a salary during academy training, and reimbursement for college courses. The least common strategies included a housing stipend, flex-

Table 2.12
Groups Targeted for Recruitment by Police Agencies

Recruitment Target ($n=105$)	Proportion
Racial/ethnic minorities	0.80
Women	0.74
College graduates	0.67
Military veterans	0.65
Prior police experience	0.53
Foreign language speakers	0.50
None	0.12
Other	0.04
Physically disabled	0.02

[4] That most agencies offer a uniform allowance suggests it may be interpreted as more of an expectation than an incentive, although it could be considered an incentive relative to other professions.

Table 2.13
Recruitment Incentives Used by Police Agencies

Recruitment Incentive ($n=106$)	Proportion
Uniform allowance	0.95
Training salary	0.82
Reimbursement for college courses	0.73
Pay rate by assignment	0.62
Salary increase for college degree	0.56
Paid academy expenses	0.45
Take-home car	0.41
Other	0.39
Tuition for external academy	0.13
Health club membership	0.13
Signing bonus	0.09
Mortgage discount	0.09
Other cash	0.08
Academy graduation bonus	0.07
Relocation expenses	0.05
Schedule preference for taking courses	0.05
None	0.01
Housing stipend	0.00

ible scheduling to account for educational courses, and relocation expenses. Nine percent of the agencies reported providing a signing bonus to applicants, while 32 percent provide cash or another award to current employees for referring a successful applicant.

Recruitment Standards

To help ensure a quality and qualified workforce, police agencies have a number of standards for applicants. The most common is education; the most common educational requirement is a high school diploma or its equivalent (Table 2.14). Relatively few require a two- or four-year college degree.

Beyond an education standard, nearly every agency required candidates to pass psychological and medical tests, possess a driver's license, and be a U.S. citizen (see Table 2.15). More than 90 percent also required candidates to pass a vision and physical agility test. Nearly 30 percent had a residency policy. Few agencies required candidates to be nonsmokers or be of a certain height or weight.

Among the most common disqualifiers (Table 2.16) reported by agencies are a suspended driver's license (93 percent), felony conviction (93 percent), and serious misdemeanor conviction (81 percent). More agencies could disqualify someone for a poor credit score (47 percent) than for any past drug use (32 percent). Nearly three in four agencies consider termination from a previous law enforcement position as a disqualification.

Table 2.14
Minimum Education Requirement for Officer Positions

Education Requirement (n=107)	Proportion
Four-year college degree	0.03
Two-year college degree	0.05
46–60 credit hours	0.11
31–45 credit hours	0.02
1–30 credit hours	0.03
High school diploma or equivalent	0.77
No formal education requirement	0.00

Table 2.15
General Requirements for Officer Positions

General Requirement (n=107)	Proportion
Psychological test	0.99
Medical test	0.99
Driver's license	0.98
U.S. citizen	0.97
Pass vision test	0.93
Physical agility test	0.91
Any age requirement	0.79
Polygraph test	0.79
No dishonorable discharge from military	0.66
Other	0.37
Local residency	0.29
Police academy graduate	0.15
Nonsmoker	0.08
Weight restrictions	0.05
None	0.02
Height restrictions	0.00

Table 2.16
Reasons Preventing an Offer of Employment as an Officer

Disqualification (n=107)	Proportion
Any misdemeanor conviction	0.19
Any serious misdemeanor conviction	0.81
Felony arrest	0.65
Felony arrest within 2 years	0.43
Felony conviction	0.93

Table 2.16—Continued

Disqualification (*n*=107)	Proportion
Prior drug use	0.32
Substance abuse arrest	0.46
Substance abuse arrest within 2 years	0.57
Substance abuse conviction	0.60
Suspended driver's license	0.93
Excessive points on driving record	0.79
Poor credit score	0.47
Termination from law enforcement	0.72
Other	0.31

Compensation

Compensation can include many components, from salary and health benefits to health-club memberships and use of take-home vehicles. Some of these items are also recruitment incentives. Here we focus on pay. Table 2.17 provides the average minimum and maximum base annual pay agencies give officers by rank. The minimum annual average base pay reported was less than $37,000 for an entry-level officer. Maximum average salaries range from more than $50,000 for officers with more than ten years of experience to more than $130,000 for the highest ranking uniformed officer.

Officers may also receive additional pay for working special assignments, shifts, or overtime, or for still some other reason. Table 2.18 summarizes total pay compensation. Not surprisingly, total pay compensation is generally higher than base annual pay (with differences in samples likely accounting for cases where it is not).[5] Among officers with at least 21 years of service, total pay is $10,000 to $15,000 higher than base pay.

---

[5]   We detected no statistically significant differences between agencies that reported total pay compensation by rank and the target population.

Table 2.17
Base Annual Pay by Rank, 2007 (in U.S. dollars)

Rank (n=102)	Minimum			Maximum		
	Median	Mean	Standard Deviation	Median	Mean	Standard Deviation
Highest ranking uniformed officer	—	—	—	133,746	130,787	55,592
All ranks below the highest ranking uniformed officer but above captain	93,009	87,654	42,423	115,066	105,411	55,409
Captain or equivalent	81.406	78,433	34,132	94,213	93,508	38,765
Lieutenant or equivalent	70,406	67,764	29,669	85,460	81,580	32,740
Sergeant, first line supervisor, or equivalent	61,976	59,722	21,390	72,863	71,494	23,813
Officer with 21 or more years of service	55,217	45,119	29,141	60,640	50,828	29,947
Officer with 11–20 years of service	53,449	45,851	27,122	59,975	51,657	28,155
Officer with 6–10 years of service	50,835	43,582	24,840	57,022	49,511	27,251
Office with 5 or less years of service	44,120	40,995	17,870	53,947	48,272	23,440
Officer, newly hired	38,955	36,713	16,210	41,718	40,488	20,855

Table 2.18
Total Pay Compensation by Rank, 2007 (in U.S. dollars)

Rank (n=63)	Minimum			Maximum		
	Median	Mean	Standard Deviation	Median	Mean	Standard Deviation
Highest ranking uniformed officer	—	—	—	142,953	146,606	59,284
All ranks below highest ranking uniformed officer but above captain	102,008	101,436	52,261	119,363	108,034	64,183
Captain or equivalent	91,280	89,739	43,517	99,194	97,419	52,383
Lieutenant or equivalent	79,697	74,315	40,171	96,215	85,299	50,592
Sergeant, first line supervisor, or equivalent	68,972	63,201	31,801	84,019	81,755	51,921
Officer with 21 or more years of service	61,506	55,539	31,217	68,199	65,200	50,152
Officer with 11–20 years of service	58,522	53,679	30,395	65,153	62,676	46,614
Officer with 6–10 years of service	56,465	50,650	27,290	63,171	58,433	41,061
Officer with 5 or fewer years of service	45,733	42,188	23,356	55,788	49,691	36,325
Officer, newly hired	37,728	35,935	20,590	41,000	36,377	26,940

NOTE: Total compensation includes base pay, special pay, overtime, and any other pay.

In 2006, three-quarters of the responding agencies indicated that they adjusted compensation. Of those adjusting compensation, 86 percent raised it for recruits (Table 2.19). Most agencies reporting an increase in recruit compensation said that it had no impact on their ability to meet their goal, but about one-third said the changes made it easier to meet the goal.

Every agency in our sample permitted their officers to work secondary or some other employment. Limits placed on such work varied by agency. While 30 percent of the agencies had no limit on outside employment, almost half limited employment by the week, and 15 percent limited it by day (only six percent limited outside employment by both week and day). The typical agency with daily limits permitted up to 12 hours per day, and those with weekly limits allowed up to 28 hours per week. Nearly one in five had some other way of limiting such employment.

Promotion

To understand how swiftly officers can move up through the chain of command, we asked each agency about the length of time officers must be employed before being eligible for promotion and how each agency determines when to offer promotional exams. On average, an officer must serve just over four years before becoming eligible for the agency's

Table 2.19
Changes in Recruit Compensation and the Ability to Meet Recruitment Goals, 2006

| Compensation Change (n=73) | Ability to Meet Goal | | | |
	Easier	No Impact	More Difficult	Total
Raised compensation	0.32	0.55	0.00	0.86
Lowered compensation	0.00	0.00	0.03	0.03
No change in compensation	0.00	0.08	0.03	0.11
Total	0.32	0.63	0.05	1.00

lowest supervisory rank position. About 94 percent of the agencies then require the officer to serve additional time, averaging two years, in this rank before being promoted to the next.

There are three typical methods for scheduling promotional exams (see Table 2.20). The most common method is scheduling a new exam when the list of those who have passed a previous exam has expired. The next most common method is to offer an exam based on a fixed time period (calendar). The third most common is to schedule exams as vacancies occur.

Retirement

Retirement systems are not uniform across agencies, but they do have some common features. Nearly every agency in our sample had a state or local retirement system or one combining the two (Table 2.21). On average, agencies reported that their officers must work about 11 years before becoming fully vested in the retirement system (Table 2.22). In the average agency, it takes 23 years of service before becoming eligible for immediate full retirement, assuming the officer has a minimum age of about 46. In their first year of retirement, officers receive an average of 54 percent of their base pay. Nearly half (43 percent) of the agencies report maintaining some kind of program to encourage officers to delay retirement (e.g., a deferred retirement option plan).

Table 2.20
Methods that Determine the Frequency of Promotional Exams

| | First Supervisor Rank (n=106) | | Second Supervisor Rank (n=107) | |
Factor	Proportion	Standard Deviation	Proportion	Standard Deviation
List expire	0.42	0.50	0.38	0.49
Calendar	0.35	0.48	0.34	0.47
Vacancy	0.23	0.42	0.24	0.43
Other	0.11	0.32	0.11	0.32

Table 2.21
Types of Agency Retirement Systems

Type (*n*=103)	Proportion
Local	0.39
State	0.47
Combined	0.14
Other	0.03

Table 2.22
Attributes of Agency Retirement Plans

Attribute	Mean	Standard Deviation
Years of service for full vestment (*n*=102)	11.30	6.95
Years of service for immediate full retirement (*n*=92)	23.00	6.54
Minimum age for full retirement (*n*=72)	46.47	11.49
% base pay in first year of retirement (*n*=80)	54.41	24.03

Current Workforce

Workforce size and distributions by sex and race/ethnicity were stable from 2006 to 2007 for the responding agencies. The average number of sworn officers was just over 1,000—about five percent less than the authorized level (Table 2.23). The average agency employed just over 300 civilians, about 10 percent less than the number authorized. In all, the agencies employed nearly one civilian for every three sworn officers. White males constituted, on average, just over 60 percent of the sworn workforce (Table 2.24).[6] In the typical agency, black males represented the next most common group (12 percent), followed by white females (nine percent).

Those at the officer rank comprise the greatest proportion of agencies' sworn workforces, about 60 percent of the average agency's sworn

---

[6]   We detected no statistically significant differences between agencies that reported the sworn workforce by race/ethnicity and sex for 2006 and 2007 and the target population.

Table 2.23
Authorized and Actual Strength by Position Type, 2006 and 2007

Strength	June 30, 2006						June 30, 2007					
	Median	Minimum	Maximum	Mean	Standard Deviation	n	Median	Minimum	Maximum	Mean	Standard Deviation	n
Authorized strength: sworn	554	271	10,215	1,097	1,479	85	595	271	10,310	1,105	1,456	90
Actual strength: sworn	552	265	9,348	1,039	1,370	84	568	259	9,399	1,046	1,346	90
Authorized strength: civilians	165	37	3,679	343	487	83	190	10	3,786	358	494	87
Actual strength: civilians	163	37	3,235	310	431	81	174	38	3,347	321	436	86

Table 2.24
Distribution of Sworn Workforce by Race/Ethnicity and Sex, 2006 and 2007

Race/Ethnicity	Male			Female		
	Median	Mean Proportion	Standard Deviation	Median	Mean Proportion	Standard Deviation
June 30, 2006 (n=72)						
White, not of Hispanic origin	0.66	0.64	0.14	0.09	0.09	0.03
Black, not of Hispanic origin	0.09	0.12	0.09	0.02	0.03	0.04
Hispanic origin, any race	0.05	0.08	0.09	0.01	0.01	0.01
Other	0.01	0.02	0.02	0.00	0.00	0.00
June 30, 2007 (n=76)						
White, not of Hispanic origin	0.66	0.62	0.15	0.09	0.09	0.04
Black, not of Hispanic origin	0.10	0.12	0.09	0.02	0.03	0.04
Hispanic origin, any race	0.05	0.09	0.11	0.01	0.01	0.02
Other	0.02	0.02	0.02	0.00	0.00	0.00

personnel (Table 2.25).[7] About 20 percent are at the first line of supervision rank (sergeant) or at a rank less than first-line supervisor but above officer.

The sworn workforce also varies in its experience, with about one in four with at least 21 years of experience (Table 2.25). As we noted earlier, the average years of service an officer must complete to become eligible for full immediate retirement is 23. These data imply that about

Table 2.25
Distribution of Sworn Workforce by Rank and Years of Service, 2007

Rank/Years of Service (n=75)	Median	Mean Proportion	Standard Deviation
Highest ranking uniformed officer	0.00	0.04	0.17
All ranks below highest ranking uniformed officer but above captain	0.01	0.05	0.15
Captain or equivalent	0.01	0.04	0.11
Lieutenant or equivalent	0.04	0.06	0.11
Sergeant, first line supervisor, or equivalent	0.12	0.12	0.09
All ranks below sergeant but above officer	0.00	0.09	0.15
Officer	0.74	0.60	0.29
1 year of service	0.06	0.07	0.07
2–5 years of service	0.17	0.16	0.10
6–10 years of service	0.19	0.18	0.09
11–15 years of service	0.18	0.19	0.10
16–20 years of service	0.14	0.15	0.09
21–25 years of service	0.09	0.14	0.15
26–30 years of service	0.06	0.09	0.16
30+ years of service	0.01	0.03	0.06

---

[7]   We detected no statistically significant differences between agencies that reported the sworn workforce by rank and years of service and the target population.

one-fourth of the workforce could retire at any time (subject to other restrictions, such as age for retirement).

Attrition

In 2007, the police agencies in our sample lost, on average, 4 percent of their sworn workforce (Table 2.26).[8] Not surprisingly, attrition was highest among line officers. The average agency lost nearly 30 line officers in 2007 (as indicated in the Mean Attrition column). The median agency lost 22 line officers (not shown in table). Mean attrition decreased with rank, being lower at higher ranks, where, presumably, there are fewer personnel. (Mean and median attrition were within one for all ranks but sergeant, for which the median agency lost three in 2007.)

Mean attrition rates (that is, the numbers of officers lost through attrition as a proportion of the total number of officers in that category) were highest at the highest ranks—a result, we surmise, of retirements. The average agency lost 6 percent of its line officers in 2007, but 12 percent of its captains and 22 percent of its highest ranking officers. (Given the low numbers of captains and high-ranking officers the median agency lost, median rates, not shown, were lower.) Yet, overall, attrition is concentrated at the lower ranks, as the Mean Proportion of Total Attrition column confirms: on average, 69 percent of attrition in 2007 was of line officers, 14 percent was of sergeants, and the rest at all other ranks.

Similarly, attrition is concentrated among those with very few or very many years of service (Table 2.27). Nearly one in five of those who depart have one year or less of experience, as indicated in the Mean Proportion of Total Attrition column. The typical agency lost 16 percent of its first-year sworn staff, as indicated by the Mean Attrition Rate category; first-year attrition reached 69 percent in one agency. At the other extreme, one in three officers lost to attrition have more than

---

[8]   We detected no statistically significant differences between agencies that reported attrition by rank and years of service and the target population.

Table 2.26
Distribution of Sworn Officer Attrition by Rank, 2007

Rank (*n*=70)	Mean Attrition	Standard Deviation	Mean Attrition Rates	Standard Deviation	Mean Proportion of Total Attrition	Standard Deviation
Highest ranking uniformed officer	0.24	0.65	0.22	0.50	0.01	0.03
All ranks below highest ranking uniformed officer but above captain	0.66	1.19	0.14	0.23	0.02	0.03
Captain or equivalent	1.10	1.33	0.12	0.17	0.04	0.05
Lieutenant or equivalent	1.87	2.79	0.04	0.05	0.04	0.04
Sergeant, first line supervisor, or equivalent	5.63	7.37	0.05	0.03	0.14	0.10
All ranks below sergeant but above officer	3.51	10.93	0.05	0.08	0.07	0.11
Officer	29.69	31.89	0.06	0.04	0.69	0.18

Table 2.27
Distribution of Sworn Officer Attrition by Years of Service, 2007

Years of Service (n=70)	Mean Attrition	Standard Deviation	Mean Attrition Rates	Standard Deviation	Mean Proportion of Total Attrition	Standard Deviation
1 year of service	7.10	10.63	0.16	0.17	0.18	0.16
2–5 years of service	4.33	5.03	0.03	0.03	0.10	0.09
6–10 years of service	4.11	7.19	0.02	0.02	0.10	0.11
11–15 years of service	3.30	3.99	0.02	0.02	0.08	0.08
16–20 years of service	3.79	4.61	0.04	0.06	0.10	0.12
21–25 years of service	6.03	9.55	0.10	0.18	0.13	0.13
26–30 years of service	7.36	12.30	0.20	0.24	0.17	0.19
30+ years of service	6.69	14.35	0.43	0.53	0.15	0.20

25 years of experience. Those with the least experience are generally new to the profession and may not find it to their taste. Those with the most experience are typically completing their career and choosing retirement.

Budgets

Police budgets vary widely by agency, but it is common for the personnel category to consume most of the operating budget. In 2006, the typical agency had 78 percent of its budget earmarked for personnel, with one agency reporting that 97 percent of its budget went to personnel. On average, agencies spent 0.27 percent of their nonpersonnel budgets on recruitment (not counting personnel costs attributed to recruitment). Some did not spend any of their operating budgets on recruitment, while others spent up to 3 percent of it on recruitment.

"Large" police organizations vary considerably in terms of their experiences, practices, and situations. Through the comparison and statistical modeling of these features, this variation can be used to develop lessons for managing police workforces. In subsequent chapters, we seek to identify lessons based on the empirical data from our survey.

CHAPTER THREE

Factors Affecting the Supply of Police Recruits

Each year, police departments throughout the United States recruit new personnel. While it is common for departments to share information with others about their programs in an effort to discern "best practices," there is little systematic analysis of characteristics of successful recruiting programs. Departments seldom collect data or implement programs in a way that rigorously controls for changes over time. Similarly, cross-department comparisons are usually descriptive and seldom use statistical techniques to control for differences in departments; that is, departments rarely conduct rigorous cross-sectional analysis.

Police recruitment practices have evolved over time. The first moves toward professionalization occurred with the 1931 recommendations of the Wickersham Commission, which advocated elimination of the spoils system (Alpert, 1991; Walker, 1997). As police agencies moved toward merit-based hiring, they faced dual problems of liability for law enforcement behavior and concerns over discrimination in police work, leading to adoption of more scientific methods in recruitment, culminating in the 1967 formation of the Law Enforcement Assistance Administration (Fyfe et al., 1997; Hogue, Black, and Sigler, 1994; Scrivner, 2006). This system was challenged in the mid-1970s when research indicated that the skills officers required for their work differed from those for which recruits were screened, trained, and tested (Goldstein, 1977). This led the Commission on Accreditation for Law Enforcement Agencies to put forth recommendations for diversifying forces. Evaluation processes today may either "select out" candidates (that is, identify flaws disqualifying candidates) or "select in" candidates (that is, identify positive qualities that make applicants attractive candidates). Controversies over these approaches and their merit have persisted throughout the community policing era (Scrivner, 2006). As a result, police recruitment is often not uniform but reflects fragmentary approaches (Orrick, 2008b; Scrivner, 2006; White and Escobar, 2008).

To identify what approaches may be most effective for police recruitment today, in this chapter, using the data from our survey, we attempt a cross-sectional analysis that controls for differing features of agencies and their communities. In particular, we explore the determinants of the supply of police recruits—why recruits join police departments—and the impact that various programs have on that supply.

Why Recruits Join Police Departments: The Basic Model

Our models rely on economic theories of occupational choice, which recognize the importance of both cash attractions, such as compensation, and noncash attractions, such as taste for particular work. Such economic models have proven to be useful for practical management. Indeed, such models have guided the military in managing its manpower needs since the advent of the all-volunteer force (see, for example, Fechter, 1970).

An Economic Model of Why Recruits Join Police Departments

An economic model holds that each potential police recruit may choose to apply or not to apply to a police department. In principle, each action carries with it a set of cash and noncash costs and benefits. The model assumes that the potential recruit chooses the specific course of action that provides the highest net cash and noncash benefits. It also assumes that potential recruits can evaluate noncash costs and benefits in cash terms. In other words, it assumes the potential recruit is able to stipulate the number of dollars of additional pay, or cash benefits, required to offset the noncash cost associated with joining the police department. Given these assumptions, we can postulate that the potential police recruit can determine a "reservation wage" making the sum of the cash and noncash benefits from joining the police department equal to the sum of that for not joining.[1] The reservation wage is the wage at which a potential recruit would be indifferent to joining or not joining the department. If the actual wage offered is above the reservation wage, the potential recruit will join the department. If it is not, the potential recruit will not join.

The wage at which a potential recruit would be willing to join a department will vary by individual differences in "taste" for or interest in police work. Individuals who are more interested in police work will be willing to accept a lower wage for it. In principle, all potential recruits may be arrayed by their reservation wages, creating a frequency distribution like that in Figure 3.1. The shaded area under the frequency distribution can be transformed into points on the police supply curve, as shown in Figure 3.2. The entire police supply curve

Figure 3.1
Frequency Distribution of Potential Recruits Classified by Their Reservation Wage

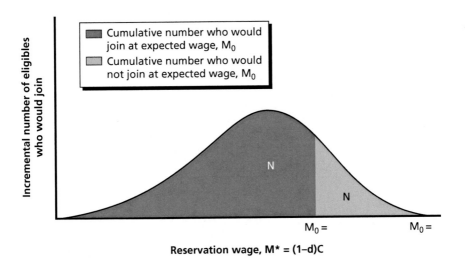

RAND MG960-3.1

---

[1]   For other examples of models using the concept of reservation wages, see Gordon and Blinder, 1980, and Eckstein and Wolpin, 1989.

Figure 3.2
Aggregate Police Supply Curve

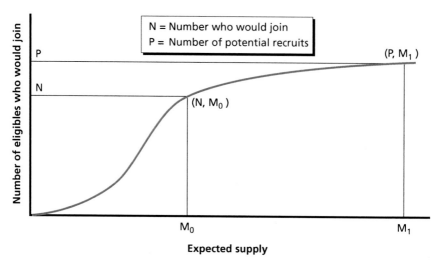

in Figure 3.2 displays the number of recruits who would be willing to join the department at each alternative police wage, other things held constant.[2]

A Simple Mathematical Model of Why Recruits Join Police Departments

In mathematical terms, we can specify the supply function as follows:

$$A = f(M, C, T, P),$$

where

A   =   number of applicants

---

[2]   If a normal curve best approximates the basic distribution of tastes, the cumulative distribution function of that curve (Figure 3.1) is the familiar upward-sloping S-shaped supply curve (Figure 3.2).

M   =   expected cash or monetary return for joining the police department

C   =   the expected cash or monetary return for not joining the police department—i.e., the opportunity cost of joining

T   =   net taste for police work

P   =   the size of the city, i.e., a scale factor.

We hypothesize that the number of recruits is a positive function of the wages offered by the police department and a negative function of the wage of nonpolice alternatives. In other words, all else equal, the higher police wages are, the more likely a potential recruit will join a police agency, but the higher nonpolice wages are, the more likely a potential police recruit will take work elsewhere. The number of police recruits will also be positively related to the net taste for police work and the scale factor, for which we use city population as a proxy. Larger cities are not only more likely to offer more varied police careers but also have more persons in the workforce.

The Basic Econometric Model

We fitted an ordinary least squares regression model using our 2007 survey and community-level data. To the above function, we added a measure of unemployment to reflect the condition of the local labor market. To measure the specific police labor market, we also added the number of vacancies. Using logarithms for each variable so as to interpret the magnitude of effects in percentage terms,[3] the wage elasticity of supply can be estimated as the coefficient α_1 in the equation

$$\text{Log applicants} = \alpha_0 + \alpha_1 \log M + \alpha_2 \log P + \alpha_3 \log C + \alpha_4 \log\_UER + \alpha_5 \log\_V + \varepsilon,$$

---

[3]   While the "double-log" model is helpful in that effects can be interpreted in percentage terms, it also assumes the elasticity coefficients remain constant at each level of the independent variables (Gujarati, 2003). Our limited sample size did not permit thorough testing of how well this functional form fit the data, but it is commonly used in models of demand and production (Greene, 2000).

where

applicants	=	number of recruits who applied
M	=	starting yearly compensation at the local police department
P	=	size of the city
C	=	average yearly compensation in all jobs in the area
UER	=	average yearly unemployment rate in the area
V	=	police department vacancies
ε	=	error term
α_1	=	$\log(\delta A/\delta M) =$ *Elasticity of supply*, which measures the percent change in the number of applicants in response to a percent change in wages offered— e.g., if α_1=10, a 10 percent change in starting compensation would result in a 10 percent change in the number of applicants.

Results for the Basic Econometric Model

Table 3.1 shows results for estimating the basic model for all applicants.[4] This model "explains" about 55 percent of the differences among police departments in our sample.

Sixty-four departments provided data that could be used to estimate a single supply curve for all applicants. Our analysis is generally consistent with economists' view of the importance of cash benefits in choosing a job. Even after accounting for the size of the cities represented in our sample and, we assume, the total number of persons looking and able to apply for police work, the compensation offered by

---

[4]   Similar to the nonresponse analyses for individual variables, we tested for systematic differences between the agencies represented in the basic model and the target population on the various agency and community characteristics. The sample was equivalent to the population on all measures except region. The proportion of agencies in the sample located in the northeastern United States was less than in the population (p = 0.10), suggesting that they were underrepresented in the sample.

Table 3.1
Econometric Results for Basic Model of Police Applicants

	Coefficient	Standard Error
Observations	64	—
R-squared	0.546	—
Log of the starting yearly compensation at the local police department	1.053***	0.382
Log of the size of the city	0.797***	0.168
Log of the average yearly compensation in all jobs in the area	0.152	0.174
Log of the average yearly unemployment rate in the area	0.330	0.254
Log of the police department vacancies	0.138	0.131
Constant	–17.226***	4.487

* indicates a statistically significant difference at $p < 0.1$; **, a significant difference at $p < 0.05$; and ***, a significant difference at $p < 0.01$.

NOTE: Coefficients are unstandardized. Neither multicollinearity nor heteroscedasticity were detected in the model.

police departments is a statistically significant explanation of the numbers of applicants. Area mean wages, a proxy for wages paid by other employers in the area, and area unemployment rates, a proxy for the general state of employment in the area, are not statistically significant.

Some measurement problems may be hiding the true relationship. We know the value of the starting yearly compensation at each department in the survey, but not the actual alternatives that prospective recruits have. General area wages and unemployment are only proxies.

It is hardly surprising to learn that police departments paying higher starting wages get more recruits. There are many examples of the importance of compensation. For example,

- In 2005 a New York City arbiter cut starting pay for New York City police officers from nearly $36,000 to $25,100 (Wilson and Grammich, 2009). By 2007, the NYPD was 2,000 recruits short of its goal of 2,800, with many new officers planning to take better-paying suburban jobs as soon as they could ("Getting Out of Dodge," 2008). A restoration of the $35,881 salary for new officers helped the department meet a reduced hiring goal of 1,250 in 2008 (Proffer, 2008).

- Arlington County, Virginia, reported meeting a four-year hiring goal and reaching full strength after increasing starting pay several times. As the department chief told a local reporter, "If we were ever going to fill these positions, we would have to improve salary competitiveness" (Armstrong, 2006). After the pay increases were approved, "We saw an immediate improvement in the quality of applicants and in the flow of applications."

Yet, when asked the effect of higher compensation on recruiting, most departments in our survey indicated that there was no effect on their ability to meet recruiting goals, even though other data provided by the departments suggested that a 10 percent increase in compensation yielded about an 11 percent increase in the number of applicants. This may indicate how difficult it is to determine or discern the impact of policy changes without an appropriate analysis of empirical data.

The positive effect of city population on police recruiting when controlling for other variables may reflect not only a greater absolute number of available potential applicants but also, as noted, a greater variety of available policing careers appealing to those with tastes for such work. We consider this further below.

Impact of the Crime Rate on Police Recruiting

Our basic model above includes only labor-market variables, such as those on compensation and unemployment. Yet the underlying theory holds that "taste" for the job also influences a recruit's decision to join a department. Taste could include the desire for adventurous or non-routine work or the desire and opportunity to make a community safer (Raganella and White, 2004; Stone and Tuffin, 2000; Slater and Reiser, 1988; Martin, 1980; Van Maanen, 1973). We cannot directly measure individual taste for or interest in police work, but we can measure some characteristics that distinguish police work, individual departments, and opportunity to help make a community safer. We might, in particular, expect local crime rates to affect recruiting police jobs. To assess the effects of crime on local police recruiting, we used three measures: rate of violent crimes per 100,000 residents, rate of property crimes, and rate of all crimes. Because, as Table 3.2 shows, these three measures of crime are highly correlated, and we wished to determine whether particular types of crime might affect recruiting, we constructed three separate models to assess their effects: one for violent crime, one for property crime, and one for total crime.

Controlling for both labor-market variables and crime rates shows that crime rates—violent, property, and total—boost recruiting.[5] Each column in Table 3.3 represents a different model: The base model does not include a crime rate, while the remaining three columns model the effect of the violent crime rate, the property crime rate, and the total crime rate on police recruiting.

More demanding, and less safe, work does not make potential recruits less inclined to be police officers but rather more inclined. As

Table 3.2
Crime Rate Correlation Matrix

	Violent Crime Rate	Property Crime Rate	Total Crime Rate
Violent Crime Rate	1	N/A	N/A
Property Crime Rate	0.7045	1	N/A
Total Crime Rate	0.8102	0.9868	1

---

5   Similar to the core regression model, the samples of agencies represented in the crime models were equivalent to the target population on all agency and community measures except region. Agencies in the northeastern United States were underrepresented ($p = 0.06$ for each model). We attempted to explore the instability of the yearly compensation variable, which was statistically significant in the models containing property and total crime rates but not the basic or violent crime–rate model. Our tests did not find multicollinearity or heteroscedasticity in any of the models. Nevertheless, when we employed bootstrapping to estimate these regression models, the yearly compensation variable was not statistically significant in any. This suggests that the instability of this variable might be due to an insufficient sample size.

Table 3.3
Econometric Results for Basic Model of Police Recruits with Crime Rates Included

	Basic Model	With Violent Crime Rate	With Property Crime Rate	With Total Crime Rate
Observations	64	61	60	60
R-squared	0.546	0.592	0.595	0.599
Log of the starting yearly compensation at the local police department (standard error)	1.053*** (0.382)	1.288*** (0.384)	1.257*** (0.375)	1.281*** (0.376)
Log of the size of the city (standard error)	0.797*** (0.168)	0.821*** (0.181)	0.834*** (0.164)	0.835*** (0.165)
Log of the average yearly compensation in all jobs in the area (standard error)	0.152 (0.174)	0.155 (0.151)	0.258* (0.141)	0.245* (0.141)
Log of the average yearly unemployment rate in the area (standard error)	0.330 (0.254)	0.073 (0.267)	0.228 (0.257)	0.186 (0.258)
Log of the police department vacancies (standard error)	0.138 (0.131)	0.080 (0.120)	0.116 (0.117)	0.108 (0.116)
Log of the crime rate (standard error)	—	0.392*** (0.126)	0.455*** (0.159)	0.488*** (0.157)
Constant (standard error)	−17.226*** (4.487)	−22.067*** (4.543)	−24.608*** (5.360)	−25.000*** (5.400)

*, **, and *** indicate a statistically significant difference at the 0.1, 0.05, and 0.01 levels, respectively, indicating that the observed difference is likely not due to chance.

NOTE: Coefficients are unstandardized. Neither multicollinearity nor heteroscedasticity were detected in the models.

with that in larger cities, perhaps police work in areas of greater crime, regardless of size, appeals more to persons with a taste for police work or a desire and opportunity to make a community safer.

Police Department Efforts to Improve Recruiting

Police departments, of course, can make their own efforts to recruit officers regardless of local conditions. We consider below tools that departments may wish to use in their recruiting, including recruiters and budgets for them, advertising, and incentives.

Recruiters and Recruiting Budget

Of the 70 departments in our survey sample, 55 have full-time recruiters. Fifteen departments had no full-time recruiters, but the average number per agency was four (Figure 3.3). On average, departments in our survey employed one recruiter per 100,000 residents, with one agency employing 14 per 100,000 residents. Statistical analysis not shown found no significant relationship between the numbers of recruiters, whether civilian or sworn officers, and of applications. We also found no evidence of a relationship between recruiting budgets and applications.

Figure 3.3
Number of Full-Time Sworn Recruiters

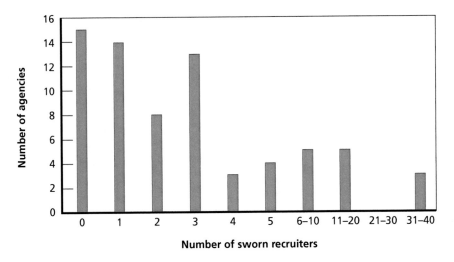

RAND *MG960-3.3*

Advertising

Departments reported using a wide variety of advertising in their recruiting efforts. Among the most common means are career fairs, Internet postings, posters, and mass media, such as newspapers, radio, and television (Figure 3.4).

To test the effects of differing forms of advertising on recruiting, we constructed a multivariate model that included labor-force variables and variables for forms of advertising that were used by 20 to 50 agencies in our sample.[6] The only advertising variable to have any statistically significant effect on recruiting was television advertising, and the effect was positive (Table 3.4).

The effect of television advertising was unexplainably large. The 0.471 coefficient translates into a 60 percent increase in applicants as a

Figure 3.4
Prevalence of Common Advertising Used by Police Departments

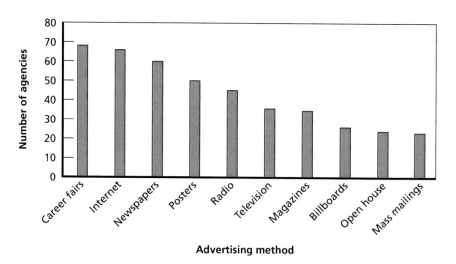

RAND *MG960-3.4*

---

[6]   We limited the number of agencies so that we could discern the effect a given form might have. We would be less able to discern the effect of a particular form of advertising used by very few or very many departments.

Table 3.4
Econometric Results for Basic Model of Police Recruits with Select Means of Advertising

	Basic Model: Total	With Common Means of Advertising
Observations	64	64
R-squared	0.546	0.606
Log of the starting yearly compensation at the local police department (standard error)	1.053*** (0.382)	1.196*** (0.397)
Log of the size of the city (standard error)	0.797*** (0.168)	0.743*** (0.185)
Log of the average yearly compensation in all jobs in the area (standard error)	0.152 (0.174)	0.210 (0.152)
Log of the average yearly unemployment rate in the area (standard error)	0.330 (0.254)	0.136 (0.285)
Log of the police department vacancies (standard error)	0.138 (0.131)	0.143 (0.129)
Magazine (standard error)	N/A	−0.028 (0.211)
Radio (standard error)	N/A	−0.360 (0.218)
Television (standard error)	N/A	0.471** (0.224)
Billboard (standard error)	N/A	0.260 (0.203)
Posters (standard error)	N/A	0.040 (0.260)
Mailings (standard error)	N/A	0.054 (0.231)
Open house (standard error)	N/A	−0.180 (0.205)
Constant (standard error)	−17.226*** (4.487)	−18.477*** (4.593)

*, **, and *** indicate a statistically significant difference at the 0.1, 0.05, and 0.01 levels, respectively, indicating that the observed difference is likely not due to chance.

NOTE: Coefficients are unstandardized. Neither multicollinearity nor heteroscedasticity were detected in the models.

result of television advertising.[7] We can conclude that other means of advertising included in our model do not appear to have been effective, but we note again that there were several methods of advertising that we did not include in our model because variation in their use, and our ability to discern their specific effects, was minimal.

Recruiting Incentives

Departments also use a wide variety of recruiting incentives. Among agencies in our sample, these included

- uniform allowance, used by 97 percent of agencies
- training salary, 84 percent
- college tuition reimbursement, 74 percent
- salary increase for degree, 60 percent
- paid academy expenses, 44 percent
- take-home car, 43 percent
- health club membership, 14 percent
- signing bonus, 14 percent
- tuition for external academy, 13 percent
- other cash bonus, 11 percent
- academy graduation bonus, 9 percent
- mortgage discount, 7 percent
- relocation expenses, 7 percent
- schedule preferences to accommodate coursework, 6 percent.

We again constructed a statistical model including labor-force variables and those incentives used by a middling range of agencies, or, more specifically, college reimbursement, salary increases for degrees, paid academy expenses, and take-home cars. We found none of the incentives to have a statistically significant effect on the number of applicants (these models also showed no signs of multicollinearity or heteroscedasticity).

---

[7]   Given that advertising is an untransformed dummy variable and "applications" is logged in this model, the percentage effect is calculated as $\exp(0.471) - 1$, which equals 60.

Recruiting by Gender and Race/Ethnicity

As noted earlier, most agencies target racial and ethnic minorities, as well as women, for special recruiting efforts. To assess the recruiting environment for male and female recruits, we constructed separate models of labor-force variables for total, male, and female recruits in the 46 departments providing all such information.[8] We found generally similar results, but a greater wage elasticity for male applicants than for the overall sample (Table 3.5). Also, compensation was statistically unrelated to female applicants. We did not find any of the advertising strategies or recruiting incentives included in our survey to have a statistically significant effect on numbers of male and female applicants (and hence do not list these in Table 3.5).

Similarly, we assessed the recruiting environment for white and nonwhite recruits, constructing separate models for each among the 47 departments that provided the necessary data (Table 3.6).[9] Again, the results were roughly similar for both groups of recruits. The wage elasticity was greater for the nonwhite applicant group than for the overall group, but wages were statistically unrelated to the number of white applicants. Further investigation is needed to explain why unemployment was inversely related to nonwhite applicants. We found none of the advertising strategies or recruiting incentives to have a statistically significant effect on the number of nonwhite applicants. We also found none of the recruiting incentives to have a statistically significant effect on the number of white applicants. We found a statistically significant negative effect of radio advertising and a statistically significant positive effect of posters on white applicants (results not shown), but the coefficients are unusually high, suggesting extremely large effects—or, more likely, the need for further analysis beyond the scope of this project to discern the true effects of these strategies.

---

[8]   The sample of agencies represented in the gender models was equivalent to the target population on all agency and community measures except region. Agencies in the Northeast region of the United States were underrepresented (p = 0.09).

[9]   As in the gender models, the sample of agencies represented in the race/ethnicity models was equivalent to the target population on all agency and community measures except region. Agencies in the Northeast were underrepresented in the sample (p = 0.08).

Table 3.5
Econometric Results for Basic Model of Police Recruits and Gender-Specific Models

	Basic Model	Base Model for Gender	Male-Only Model	Female-Only Model
Observations	64	46	46	46
R-squared	0.546	0.582	0.491	0.406
Log of the starting yearly compensation at the local police department (standard error)	1.053*** (0.382)	1.354*** (0.475)	2.072* (1.191)	1.633 (1.569)
Log of the size of the city (standard error)	0.797*** (0.168)	0.752*** (0.212)	0.547* (0.312)	0.521 (0.404)
Log of the average yearly compensation in all jobs in the area (standard error)	0.152 (0.174)	0.139 (0.186)	−0.345 (3.397)	−0.326 (4.832)
Log of the average yearly unemployment rate in the area (standard error)	0.330 (0.254)	0.225 (0.320)	−1.100 (0.945)	−1.093 (1.077)
Log of the police department vacancies (standard error)	0.138 (0.131)	0.169 (0.168)	0.228 (0.231)	0.398 (0.326)
Constant (standard error)	−17.226*** (4.487)	−19.709*** (5.153)	−18.124 (27.758)	−15.573 (39.539)

*, **, and *** indicate a statistically significant difference at the 0.1, 0.05, and 0.01 levels, respectively, indicating that the observed difference is likely not due to chance.

NOTE: Coefficients are unstandardized. Multicollinearity was not detected in the models. Heteroscedasticity was detected in the male- and female-specific models so we adjusted the standard errors in these models based on procedures outlined by Davidson and MacKinnon (1993).

Table 3.6
Econometric Results for Basic Model of Police Recruits and Race-Specific Models

	Basic Model	Basic Model for Race	Model for White Recruits	Model for Nonwhite Recruits
Observations	64	47	47	47
R-squared	0.546	0.582	0.307	0.492
Log of the starting yearly compensation at the local police department (standard error)	1.053*** (0.382)	1.349*** (0.475)	1.623 (1.327)	2.624*** (0.800)
Log of the size of the city (standard error)	0.797*** (0.168)	0.750*** (0.212)	0.327 (0.398)	0.810** (0.380)
Log of the average yearly compensation in all jobs in the area (standard error)	0.152 (0.174)	0.136 (0.184)	−0.323 (3.478)	−0.554 (0.354)
Log of the average yearly unemployment rate in the area (standard error)	0.330 (0.254)	0.208 (0.315)	−1.074 (1.286)	−1.345* (0.729)
Log of the police department vacancies (standard error)	0.138 (0.131)	0.173 (0.167)	0.326 (0.268)	0.233 (0.257)
Constant (standard error)	−17.226*** (4.487)	−19.590*** (5.133)	−11.713 (28.473)	−25.632*** (8.689)

*, **, and *** indicate a statistically significant difference at the 0.1, 0.05, and 0.01 levels, respectively, indicating that the observed difference is likely not due to chance.

NOTE: Coefficients are unstandardized. Multicollinearity was not detected in the models. Heteroscedasticity was detected in the model for white recruits, so we adjusted the standard errors in this model based on procedures outlined by Davidson and MacKinnon (1993).

CHAPTER FOUR

Career Management

While a great deal of attention has been paid to recruiting new police officers, recruiting is just one facet of managing police personnel. How officers progress through their careers is important both to themselves and to the departments they serve. Progression determines the jobs officers can do and the compensation for them. If they progress too quickly, they may not have the experiences they need to do the jobs they are promoted to do. If they progress too slowly, officers may become frustrated and may leave for other departments. Job satisfaction is often related to meeting an officer's expectation of progress through the department hierarchy. An optimal rate of progression will meet the needs of individual officers and of the department.

For departments, how officers progress will determine the experience and quality of their agency at various ranks, as well as the personnel costs of the department. For the departments, there is an optimal year-of-service profile that reflects the distribution of police ranks. Ideally, departments know what experience they want at each grade and what would be a steady flow of officers through the ranks. While police departments are similar to military organizations in these characteristics, they are also more constrained than military systems. Military systems are often characterized as "up-or-out" systems, while police departments are "stay, if up or not" (i.e., officers can complete an entire career within one rank or can be promoted) systems. Military systems refresh their ranks through selective promotions and forcing out those not promoted out (for more on military systems, see Rostker, 2006, especially pp. 237–243). Police systems refresh their ranks through voluntary attrition, which can be influenced by personnel policies. Yet, while the means of each system may be different, the goals are the same: to maintain a force profile that motivates young officers to move ahead to more senior jobs.

Each department lives with past personnel decisions as past recruit *cohorts* progress through the system. Past hiring freezes, for example, can reverberate over time, creating shortages of candidates for promotion in future years. Such shortages reduce the selectivity the department has in promoting officers. Selectivity can help ensure that future leaders are of the quality the department wants and have the experiences the department needs. Promoting officers too young will not only mean that leaders may lack experience necessary for their jobs but also that subsequent cohorts may not have the opportunities for promotion. Young officers promoted early stay in place for extended periods of time. Understanding the relationship between the ideal years-of-service/experience profile and policies affecting the profile is essential to good personnel planning.[1]

Modeling the Police Department

The movement of personnel through very large systems—whether a police department, a military service system, or other "social system"—can often be modeled as a Markovian process (Merck and Hall, 1971). Doing a full modeling of individual police departments required more data than we were able to obtain through our survey. We approximated the results of a Markovian analysis by asking departments to indicate the proportion of officers at a number of year-of-service benchmark cells and interpolated between the benchmark cells. Figure 4.1 shows the average distribution for departments answering these questions. This average profile is similar to the optimal year-of-service profiles for a hierarchical "closed" organization with large numbers of junior

---

[1] Deliberate personnel planning in hierarchical organizations has a rich history that can be traced to at least 1679, when the Secretary of the Admiralty in Britain began regulating the annual entry of officers into the Royal Navy. By 1779, the Royal Marines were managing career structures, retention rates, and promotion probabilities (Smith, 1968, p. 258).

Figure 4.1
Average Years-of-Service Profile

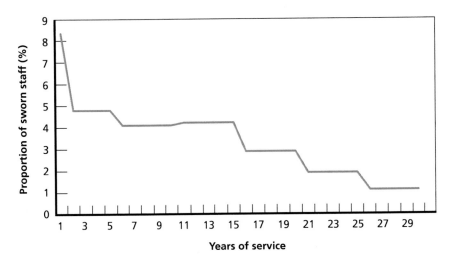

personnel and progressively fewer senior personnel.[2] In such organizations, attrition each year reduces the size of the surviving cohort.

The "average" profile hides substantial variation among departments. Departments that have this "desirable" profile are easier to manage compared to those that do not. For these departments, yearly recruitment patterns tend to be very stable, with a reasonably predictable number of officers moving through the ranks each year. Departments with this profile most likely provide career opportunities attuned to their grade structure. Departments without this profile move between "boom" and "bust" as cohorts of different sizes progress through the system. At one point in time, the average patrol officer in such departments may have as little as four years of service; at another, as many as twelve. This means that the cost and level of experience of the patrol force will vary over time, raising questions of the cost of experience.

---

[2]   A closed organization is one that accepts few lateral transfers, in which most personnel with little or no experience move up through the ranks over time.

To better understand variation among departments, we categorized the data into three variables: percentage of officers in the first decade of service, with a mean value of 48 percent; percentage of officers in the second decade of service, with a mean value of 36 percent; and percentage of officers in the third decade of service, with a mean value of 17 percent.

To illustrate the problems departments may have when the ratios among these three age groups become unbalanced, we constructed Figure 4.2. This figure illustrates "healthy" and "unhealthy" age/experience profiles among the agencies.

Agency A has a pattern consistent with the average of all agencies, which is relatively healthy. The proportion of staff in each cohort is proportionally less than the previous one. The remaining agencies exhibit patterns that may contribute to management problems. Because the total for the three decades must equal 100 percent, an increase in one category means a decrease in at least one of the others.

Figure 4.2
"Healthy" and "Unhealthy" Distributions of Officers by Decade of Service

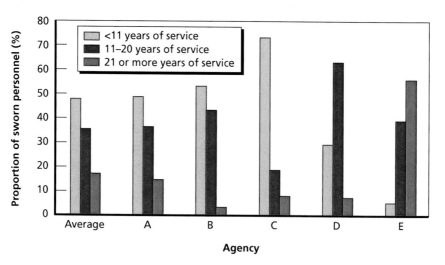

Agency B has a very low proportion of officers in the most senior cohort, suggesting that the agency may suffer from a lack of experienced officers who can provide supervision and leadership to others.

Agency C has an extremely large junior cohort. The problem of having fewer senior officers in this agency is exacerbated by the size of the junior cohort and the corresponding greater need for training, mentoring, and supervision. Further difficulties might arise as these officers retire and are replaced with even younger officers. Some junior personnel may need to fill leadership positions, but many, given competition within their cohort, will have little prospects for promotion. This might make those not promoted question their long-term commitment to the agency.

Agency D has a very large mid-level cohort. This might contribute to future challenges in choosing low- and mid-level supervisors. The cost of personnel will also substantially increase as this large cohort progresses into the senior cohort.

Agency E has an extremely small junior cohort and extremely large senior cohort. Given that more experienced officers are paid more than junior officers, the cost of personnel for this agency would be much greater than that for others. This agency might also find it difficult to find young talent to cultivate and promote into leadership positions. As its senior cohort begins to retire, it will lose a large amount of experience and its profile will likely "flip" as the large senior cohort is replaced by a large junior cohort. This might create difficulties in training, mentoring, supervision, and career progression.

To illustrate how these distributions varied throughout the sample, we provide Figures 4.3 and Figure 4.4. Figure 4.3 shows departments whose first decade force was larger than the mean of our sample and the corresponding impact on the other parts of the age/experience profile. On the extreme right of the figure are departments with large cohorts of junior personnel. As noted above, these departments will have problems training, mentoring, and supervising new recruits, given a lack of senior personnel.

Most departments that had more officers in their first decade did so to compensate for the lack of officers in their second decade (25 percent) or in the third decade (38 percent). In a number of cases, the

Figure 4.3
Distribution of Officers by Decade of Service Among Agencies with Higher Proportions of Officers in the First Decade of Service

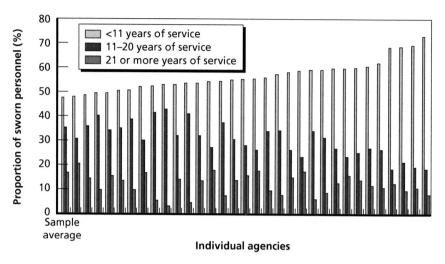

Figure 4.4
Distribution of Officers by Decade of Service Among Agencies with Lower Proportions of Officers in the First Decade of Service

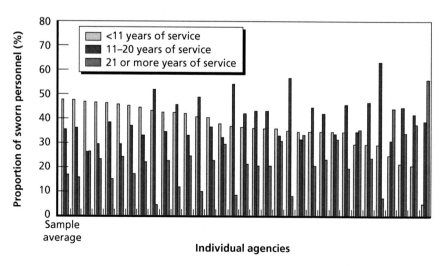

larger number of first-decade officers reflected the shortage of more senior officers in both the second and third decades (28 percent).

Figure 4.4 shows distributions of officers by decade of service among departments with lower proportions of officers in their first decade. In the most extreme cases, as senior officers retire, less-experienced cohorts will not suffice to fill their ranks, and the average age of the force will decrease. This may be appropriate, but if the size of the first-decade force is too small, it will not be able to sustain the desired year-of-service/grade standards.

A majority of the departments that had fewer officers in their first decade did so to compensate for the larger number of officers in their second decade (6 percent) or in the third decade (16 percent). Six departments not only had fewer first-decade officers, but also had fewer second-decade officers, as well as a very large number of officers in their third decade. Conversely, five departments had higher numbers of second-decade officers and lower number of third-decade officers (22 percent). In a number of cases, the smaller number of first-decade officers reflected the larger number of more-senior officers in both the second and third decades (21 percent).

Departments with cohorts that substantially differ from the typical may find it difficult to control yearly fluctuations in their personnel profiles. Once a personnel system starts to oscillate, efforts centered on filling vacancies with new recruits will not dampen the oscillations. In order to gain control of the system, the departments will need to take steps to dampen the oscillations by changing the normal attrition patterns or fill the year-of-service/experience voids by hiring experienced officers from other departments.

Controlling attrition can be tricky and costly and is not always successful. For example, during the early 1990s drawdown of military personnel at the end of the Cold War, the military services took very different paths. The Air Force cut off recruiting, leading to an oscillation that took a decade to correct and resulted in periods of boom and bust for such groups as pilots (Grissmer and Rostker, 1992; Rostker, 2006, especially pp. 639–643).

Attrition among less-experienced police officers who do not have a substantial stake in their department can be particularly difficult to control. These officers can leave for other jobs that pay better or have better benefits. Officers who have served in a department for some period of time have built up seniority "benefits" in ways that are both formal and informal. Leaving a department to start over with another department may mean that those departments may offer such benefits as being able to pick duty assignments, for example.

CHAPTER FIVE

Evidence-Based Lessons for Personnel Planning

Police agencies may face many constraints in what they can do to recruit, retain, and manage personnel. For example, while our analysis, not surprisingly, found compensation to be among the strongest predictors of a department's ability to attract personnel, agencies do not control monies available for salaries. It is also important to note that the candidates attracted by higher compensation might not be the most qualified or have the attributes (e.g., service orientation or communication skills) most desired by agency leaders.

Police agencies undertake many initiatives to recruit, retain, and manage their personnel. Many have recruiting budgets and full-time recruiting staff. Many also target specific groups, such as women or racial and ethnic minorities, for recruitment in order to meet policy or other needs. Virtually all offer some form of recruitment incentive, though virtually all also have some requirements that disqualify some potential applicants. Agencies also advertise for recruits in many ways. Yet most of these tactics appear to have no effect. We found little evidence that differences in advertising strategies, incentives, or numbers of recruiters, for example, affect how many recruits a department can attract. Some tactics, such as raising compensation, appear to attract candidates but were largely dismissed by those responding to our survey. In many ways, these findings are inconsistent with what has been found to facilitate military recruiting (Rostker, 2006; Wilson and Grammich, 2009). Compensation (pay and bonuses, both in-kind and cash) makes a difference, but so too do effective advertising and recruiters. In fact, the military goes to great lengths to test and understand how best to maximize the effectiveness of these various strategies (e.g., the Marine Corps examines multiple measures of effectiveness for specific advertisements, such as ad recall and action taken because of ads, and lead-generation variables, such as qualified leads, conversation rates, and recruiter support). Additional analysis needs to be conducted to understand if the police profession is fundamentally different from the military and these strategies simply do not work for it, or if the strategies work but are implemented in such a way that it is difficult to detect a measureable effect (e.g., advertisements have too little dosage, have an inappropriate message, or are not focused on or directed to the right audience; recruiters do not have effective training or incentives).

Many variables affecting recruitment and retention are outside the control of agencies. Our analysis also found city size—an indicator, we believe, for career opportunities and absolute number of applicants likely to be available—to positively influence the attractiveness of an agency to recruits. Yet city size is not something policymakers can easily control, and are most unlikely to do so for the purpose of attracting more police officers. Controlling for all other variables, higher crime rates appear to attract rather than repel candidates, perhaps indicating that such areas are attractive to candidates with a taste for police work or a desire to help make communities safer. Yet this, too, is certainly something neither agencies nor policymakers would seek to manipulate for the sake of attracting candidates (although marketing could focus on career opportunities that relate to "taste" for police work and ability to "make a difference"). Some variables affecting management of force profiles are also outside the control of agencies or policymakers. For example, variables affecting the size of cohorts progressing through a system, including birth rates and economic conditions by year, are outside the control of policymakers. Others, such as pension qualifications, are outside the control of police agencies. Agencies may also operate under constraints of collective bargaining agreements or legal hiring restrictions.

The results of the statistical analysis were less robust than we had hoped. While we had hoped to include in the analysis most of the departments surveyed, many did not respond, and those that did respond often provided incomplete data. In total, we had information from only 70 departments that we used to estimate our basic model. The number was substantially reduced when the data were disaggregated by race and gender. Often we were not able to make the best use of data because information provided was internally inconsistent and complementary data were missing. In some cases only categorical data, e.g., binary or dummy variables (that is, a variable in which presence of something is coded as "1" and its absence is coded as "0," of which a yes/no variable would be an example), provided information and subsequent results that were hard to understand. For example, the model of police recruits suggested that television was positively associated with applicants; however, its effect was quite large. A larger sample and better information might give more insight on its effect on recruiting.

The information on career profiles was very interesting, and the variation across departments suggests that there are many departments that face significant management challenges. Fully analyzing these challenges would require much more detailed data than we were able to collect. Such data can only be collected by archiving and processing "snapshots" over time of standard personnel files. Better data and testing of recruitment and retention strategies, with a simultaneous focus on assessing their implementation, can help agencies better manage these challenges by employing practices shown to work, limiting those that are untested, and avoiding those not supported by rigorous evaluation.

The individual regression results did not identify specific strategies and incentives associated with increases in the number of applicants. The results did, however, strongly confirm the importance of compensation, as suggested by the basic economic model.

Improving Personnel Planning

There is growing recognition that advances in criminal justice theory and practice require the analysis of data and evidence (Walker, 2006; Maguire, 2004; Maguire and King, 2004; Clear and Frost, 2007). The success of various problem-based interventions (e.g., Braga, 2001; McGarrell et al., 2001; McGarrell et al., 2002; Kennedy et al., 2001;

Eck and Spelman, 1987; Clarke and Goldstein, 2002) highlights the kinds of achievements that can be made through the direct use of data and analysis. Unfortunately, there are numerous challenges to using police administrative data (Uchida and King, 2002; Langworthy, 2002; Sherman and Glick, 1984; Maguire et al., 1998; Uchida et al., 1986; Archbold and Maguire, 2002; Fyfe, 2002; Maguire and Schulte-Murray, 2001). Our survey and the process of its administration highlighted a number of these for analysis, evidence-based personnel planning, and the promulgation of data-driven staffing lessons.

What We Learned About Personnel Data Limitations

More than one in four police agencies with 300 or more officers did not respond to our survey. More than one in ten of those that responded failed to complete at least 80 percent of the questions. Agencies had trouble providing basic personnel facts and attributes. Through analysis of response patterns, we discerned that the greatest difficulty concerned the size of the recruitment budget, the number of officers by rank and years of service, and attrition by rank and years of service. Agencies often provided inconsistent data, evident from analysis of responses to multiple questions on numbers of staff and applicants and levels of compensation.

Although we tested for (and did not find) distinguishing characteristics of agencies failing to submit a survey, we cannot determine why a particular agency did not respond to the survey, did not answer every question, or provided inconsistent results. Nor can we determine what accounts for nonresponse to a particular item or inconsistencies among agencies. Discerning such detail would require extensive follow-up with all of the agencies in the population. Nevertheless, we have anecdotal information about these issues based on many discussions we had with respondents as we provided technical assistance. They highlighted three categories of difficulties: limits to data accessibility, scarcity of resources, and narrow data collection scope.

Limits to Data Accessibility. For some agencies, information was not electronic, so providing information, especially by time or another variable, involved the physical examination and analysis of files—a monumental task. For others, electronic data were available, but respondents could not access it or make the queries we requested. Some agencies purge or store data in operational databases, complicating access to it. These problems were exacerbated when only one or a small number of persons had the ability, authority, and knowledge to access the data and were further exacerbated when these persons were outside the police agency and had other agencies to serve.

Data compilation also complicated response. Most agencies do not maintain a single database with all personnel information. This requires aggregating data from multiple sources. This adds obvious transaction costs, such as the need for more time and involvement of additional staff, when the databases are spread across organizational units, such as the academy, recruitment unit, and the personnel bureau. This becomes even more challenging when the data are housed in other units of local government, such as a city personnel department that administers staff for the entire city. When administrative data are compiled and housed outside the direct control of the police department, additional effort is required to coordinate and complete the task. Often multiple databases exist that cannot be aggregated into a single source of information. This complicates the ability to perform queries that require more than a single variable.

Scarcity of Resources. Perhaps the most obvious explanation for nonresponse is scarcity of resources. Given demands on staff, police agencies have a difficult enough time collecting data, let alone collating and providing data for external purposes. This could result in agencies not responding at all or simply responding to the questions that are easiest to answer. Lack of resources may also explain the difficulty of overcoming data access problems noted above. Staff who could overcome these problems have limited time, and there are limited financial resources for technical innovations to overcome them.

Narrow Data Collection Scope. Some departments do not collect specific personnel information about their staff and organization. Why they did not do so—whether because of lack of resources, belief that it has little utility, or lack of consideration—was never evident.

Developing an Infrastructure for Evidence-Based Personnel Planning

The development and application of basic, evidence-based tenets of police personnel management (i.e., basing decisions on data and analysis as opposed to random choices, anecdotes, or precedent) are hampered by data limitations and limited analytical investment. Accounting for the changing context of police staffing and improving the effectiveness and efficiency of police workforces requires police leaders to

- commit to evidence-based personnel planning and decisionmaking, gathering data on recruiting, retention, and variables likely to affect them
- distinguish workforce structures from levels and set goals for their most cost-effective workforce profile
- acknowledge that the determinants of the demand for and supply of police personnel are *multidimensional, systemic,* and *local,* which challenges the ability to meet workforce goals
- understand that recruitment and retention strategies should help agencies attain both the proper level and structure for their workforce
- recognize the importance of compensation in attracting workers
- maintain workforce balances and avoid oscillation of workforce structures (e.g., suddenly shifting from a predominantly senior force to a predominantly junior one)
- expand, integrate, and streamline personnel data systems
- partner within and across governments to leverage time and expertise on workforce issues

These local efforts can be bolstered by national efforts. Chief among them would be leadership and support in the development of an ongoing national data collection effort that can facilitate comparative and longitudinal analyses of police staffing. Because data without analysis are of little value, support for local and national analysis would also be necessary to derive lessons for the law enforcement community. Analysis could focus on assessing if, when, how, and under what circumstances recruitment and retention strategies work, the career and personal needs of officers are met, and the administrative goals of management are accomplished. Among others, the National Institute of Justice and other units of the Department of Justice (e.g., Bureau of Justice Assistance, Office of Community Oriented Policing Services) may be equipped to provide resources for or guidance to local efforts. Such support might include centralizing and standardizing data collection systems (and expanding them where they exist); targeting resources where they are likely to prove most effective; facilitating pilot projects to test comprehensive, real-time data collection and analysis programs (not just survey-based programs, which are difficult to use to capture critical personnel data, but other cost-effective formats that permit more detailed analysis, such as master personnel file templates); and disseminating lessons of what has worked well in differing jurisdictions. Similar to the U.S. Department of Defense Manpower Data Center, these efforts could be facilitated, administered, and evaluated by a National Police Personnel Data Center.

Police Recruitment and Retention Survey Procedures

The sampling frame for our survey was the 2007 National Directory of Law Enforcement Administrators (NDLEA). The NDLEA is a standard, comprehensive list of police agencies that has been used as the sampling frame for national surveys in previous studies that have passed rigorous peer review (Jordan et al., 2009; Davis, et al., 2006; Taylor et al. 2006; Riley et al., 2005; Davis et al., 2004; Gilmore Commission, 2003).

We began by developing and testing the survey instrument. We derived questions from three primary sources: (1) our knowledge of and experience with large personnel systems in policing, the military, and the federal government; (2) the instruments used and issues explored in previous surveys and studies relating to police staffing issues, including Taylor et al. (2006), the 2003 Law Enforcement Management and Administrative Statistics survey (U.S. Department of Justice, 2006), and Koper, Maguire, and Moore (2002); and (3) discussions with police practitioners. Once drafted, we tested the questionnaire in late 2007 with five large police departments: Columbus, Ohio; Las Vegas, Nevada; Dallas, Texas; New Orleans, Louisiana; and Pittsburgh, Pennsylvania.

We collected initial feedback on the survey instrument through face-to-face meetings in Pittsburgh and Dallas with sworn and civilian staff having personnel administration responsibilities. Our second round of testing involved sending email to the contact person in the Columbus and Las Vegas departments to briefly explain the study and request assistance with questionnaire development. Once these departments agreed, we mailed a paper-and-pencil questionnaire to the contact person for completion. We also asked the contact person to note any comments on problem questions, confusing terms, or insufficient answer choices. After receiving the completed questionnaire, we called the contact person to discuss the responses and comments to the survey. We conducted a final face-to-face round of testing with the departments in New Orleans and Pittsburgh.

After discussions with all five test departments and further revisions by the project team, we finalized the questionnaire in February 2008. Preliminary testing helped refine the question wording and concepts, especially for assessing the issues of interest to us. The final survey contained 46 items and a number of subitems. Appendix B provides the full final version of the questionnaire.

To ensure an acceptable response rate, we developed a comprehensive nonresponse protocol, provided ample field time so that departments could take time to compile information and respond, and provided significant one-on-one technical assistance to agencies as they completed the survey. We began by sending each department a full survey packet with the instrument, letters of endorsement from RAND and the National Institute of Justice, and a postcard to request contact information for survey follow-up. We mailed the initial packet on February 27, 2008; mailed another copy of the packet to nonrespondents again on April 8, 2008; and then sent the packet yet again (by FedEx) on May 19, 2008. We also called nonrespondents about a week and a half after each mailing, confirming that the packet had been received, encouraging completion as soon as possible, and answering any questions. The widely varying ways in which cities and police departments compile personnel data led to many questions about the survey and the amount of time to complete it. We sent a final reminder to nonrespondents on August 20, 2008, with follow-up calls on September 23 and 24. Altogether, the survey was in the field for 38 weeks.

Our sample was the 146 departments in the United States with at least 300 sworn officers. Altogether, we received 107 completed surveys (six departments refused, and the remainder provided no contact or information). This equates to a 73 percent response rate, which is favorable, given the complexity of the survey. We compared character-istics of those that responded, our sample, to those of our target popu-lation based on data we had available for all agencies (see Table A.1). Respondents were equivalent on all available measures: size of agency and community, region, annual wage earned in the community, unem-ployment, and violent and property crime.

Some responding departments had trouble completing various sections of the survey. About 12 percent of the departments failed to complete at least 80 percent of the questions. To further assess problem

Table A.1
Comparison of Respondents to the Target Population

	Target Population		Respondents		Difference	
	Value	Observations	Value	Observations	Value	P-Value
Sworn officers (mean)	1,300	146	1,350	107	−50	0.92
Population (mean)	433,521	143	456,444	106	−22,924	0.83
Northeast region (%)	16	146	14	107	2	0.60
Midwest region (%)	12	146	14	107	−2	0.69
Southeast region (%)	25	146	24	107	1	0.85
South region (%)	19	146	19	107	0	0.92
West region (%)	27	146	29	107	−2	0.69
Annual community wage (mean)	40,373	133	40,357	99	15	0.99
Unemployment rate (mean)	5	145	5	107	0	0.90
Violent crime rate (mean)	932	141	910	104	22	0.72
Property crime rate (mean)	5,303	141	5,081	103	222	0.34

areas, we categorized questions of the survey to assess nonresponse by substantive section. Table A.2 shows the percentage of departments that failed to complete at least half of each substantive section (see the survey instrument in Appendix B for the corresponding survey questions). It shows that departments had the most trouble answering questions about recruitment costs, departmental statistics, and attrition. We provide the sample size corresponding to the analyses throughout this report so as to make clear the number of departments on which the results are based.

We compared the agencies that completed at least half of each substantive section to those that did not to learn if there was a systematic difference that might explain why an agency willing to submit a response did not complete a specific section (tables not shown). As

Table A.2
Survey Nonresponse by Substantive Section

Substantive Section	Corresponding Survey Questions	Percentage of Departments Not Completing at Least Half of the Section
General recruitment and hiring	1, 2	3%
Statistics on hiring	3, 4, 5, 6, 7, 8, 9, 10, 11, 12	1%
Recruitment strategies	13, 14, 15, 16, 17	2%
Recruitment incentives	18, 19	2%
Recruitment costs	20	31%
Recruitment standards	21, 22, 23	0%
Unions	24	0%
Compensation and benefits	25, 26, 27, 28, 29, 30, 31	4%
Promotion possibilities	32, 33, 34, 35	2%
Retirement	36, 37, 38, 39	3%
Departmental statistics	40, 41, 42	20%
Attrition	43, 44, 45	21%

in the other nonresponse analyses, we tested by size of agency and community, region, annual wage earned in the community, unemployment, and violent and property crime. We found no evidence of systematic variation for general recruitment and hiring, recruitment strategies, or recruitment incentives. Those failing to provide information on recruitment costs were less likely to be in the Western United States (p = 0.10). Larger agencies (p = 0.00), those in larger communities (p = 0.00), and those in the South (p=0.10) were less likely to provide information about compensation and benefits. Similarly, larger agencies (p = 0.00) and those in larger communities (p = 0.00) had more difficulty providing information on promotion possibilities and retirement, whereas agencies in the South (p = 0.06) had greater difficulty offering departmental statistic information. Larger agencies (p = 0.07), but not those in larger communities, were less likely to provide information about attrition. Differences for statistics on hiring, recruitment standards, and unions were irrelevant, as all or all but one provided this information.

Many agencies also had difficulty reporting consistent information. This was evident in our checks of staffing levels, applicants, and compensation. For 2007, we asked respondents to provide their sworn staffing level in three different ways: overall, by rank and years of service, and by race/ethnicity and gender. Of those that provided data, only 18 percent provided the same total in the questions pertaining to sworn officers by rank and years of service and sworn officers overall, while 16 percent did not provide an overall value that was within 50 percent of the value provided by rank and years of service. Similarly, only 13 percent provided the same total in the questions pertaining to sworn officers by rank and years of service and sworn officers by race/ethnicity and gender, while another 13 percent did not provide a value by race/ethnicity and gender that was within 50 percent of the value provided by rank and years of service. There was also inconsistency between the value provided for applicants overall and applicants by race/ethnicity and gender. Of those reporting 2007 data, only 39 percent reported the same value for both questions. Fifteen percent of the agencies did not report a value for total applicants that was within 30 percent of the value provided for applicants by race/ethnicity and gender. Finally, we asked respondents to provide values of both base-line and total compensation (including base pay, special pay, and over-time) by rank/years of service. Forty-six percent of those providing data reported that they had at least one category of rank/years of service with total compensation that was less than its baseline compensation.

It is important to keep these data limitations in mind when considering the results of this study. While we attempt to minimize their effects as much as possible, such as by excluding cases with nonsensical values, it is clear that measurement problems pervade police personnel data. The challenges encountered in this survey provide an excellent opportunity to highlight critical problems in police personnel data systems, which we discussed in the concluding chapter.

Survey Instrument

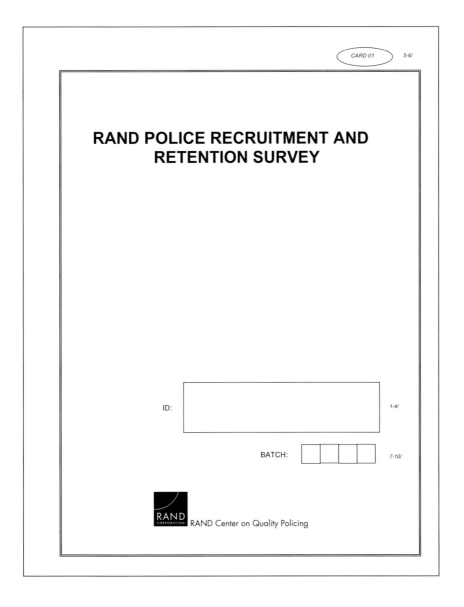

CARD 01   5-6/

RAND POLICE RECRUITMENT AND RETENTION SURVEY

ID: 1-4/

BATCH: 7-10/

RAND   RAND Center on Quality Policing

BACKGROUND INFORMATION

In response to calls from the law enforcement community, the RAND Center on Quality Policing is conducting a survey of local police departments to provide the law enforcement community with evidence-based lessons for improving recruitment and retention. This study is being conducted with support from the U.S. Department of Justice (see attached letter of support). RAND is a non-partisan, nonprofit research institution that conducts independent, objective research and analysis to advance public policy.

We are asking you to participate in the attached survey about the recruitment and retention of officers in your department. This survey is completely voluntary, and you may choose not to answer a specific question for any reason. There is no penalty if you choose not to respond. However, we strongly encourage your participation, as responses from your department and others across the nation are necessary to ensure we have a representative sample upon which to provide the law enforcement community with concrete, actionable, data-driven lessons backed up by many departments. To ensure your response can be represented in our analysis, we request that you return your completed survey within one month of receipt.

We are not requesting any individually identifiable data. Any data presented about personnel in a department will be offered in summary form and will not be portrayed to identify a person in any way. This research has been reviewed by RAND's Institutional Review Board, which is responsible for ensuring the protection of human subjects in RAND's projects. All aspects of the project are continuously reviewed as part of RAND's comprehensive quality assurance process.

If you have any questions about this survey, please feel free to write to us at PDRR@rand.org and we will respond to you as soon as possible. You may also contact the lead researcher and Associate Director of the Center on Quality Policing, Dr. Jeremy Wilson, at 412-683-2300 x4462 or jwilson@rand.org.

In this survey, you will be asked to provide information about your agency's experience with recruiting, hiring, and retaining officers. You are being asked to consult your agency's records of these activities in order to be able to report on the hiring pipeline for 2006 and 2007. You may wish to review the entire survey before you begin in order to familiarize yourself with the type of information being requested and to determine who in your organization may need to assist in completing the survey.

To thank you for your time in responding, we will provide you a copy of the report upon completion of the analysis. The report will provide benchmark metrics and data-driven lessons that your agency should find useful in planning for your agency's recruitment and retention needs.

2

RECRUITMENT AND HIRING

For the purposes of this survey, "officer" means a police officer in a sworn position.

Any question in this survey that asks you to answer regarding a specific year (primarily 2006 and/or 2007) may be answered either based on that calendar year or based on that fiscal year. In either case, however, we ask that wherever possible you keep your reporting consistent with whichever method you select.

1. **Before beginning this survey, please take a look at questions 3-11 on pages 2-4 and question 15 on page 6. In these questions, you will be asked to report on agency recruitment and hiring during 2006 and 2007. For this survey, will you be reporting these numbers by:**
    (Mark One)

    ₁☐ Calendar Year, or   11/

    ₂☐ Fiscal Year?

2. **Is your agency under any sort of legal hiring restriction, such as a Federal consent decree or court order?**
    (Mark One)

    ₁☐ No   12/

    ₂☐ Yes

STATISTICS ON HIRING

3. **Did your agency have any form of hiring goal (in number of new hires) for 2006?** *By hiring goal, we mean the number of new officers for which you were aiming.*

    ₁☐ If No → 3a. Which of the following applied to your agency, if any? *(Mark All That Apply)*   13/

    > ₁☐ We had no vacancies   14/

    > ₂☐ We had no authorization to hire (e.g., hiring freeze)   15/

    > ₃☐ We hired anyone qualified   16/

    ₂☐ If Yes → 3b. What was the goal, in numbers? ☐☐☐☐☐   17-21/

    > 3c. On what attribute(s) was your agency's goal based? *(Mark All That Apply)*

    > ₁☐ Fill vacancies   22/

    > ₂☐ Race/Ethnicity   23/

    > ₃☐ Sex   24/

    > ₄☐ Education   25/

    > ₅☐ Prior military experience   26/

    > ₆☐ Prior police experience   27/

    > ₇☐ Other *(please specify)* _____   28-29/

                                                                        CARD 01

3

4. How many total applicants <u>applied</u> to your agency for sworn officer positions during 2006 and 2007? *By "applied" we mean formally submitted an application.*

	2006	2007	
Total number of applicants	☐☐☐☐	☐☐☐☐	30-37/

5. How many sworn officers were hired during 2006 and 2007?

	2006	2007	
Total number of applicants hired	☐☐☐☐	☐☐☐☐	38-45/

6. How many of the officers hired during 2006 and 2007 had:

	2006	2007	Don't Know	
prior civilian law enforcement experience?	☐☐☐☐	☐☐☐☐	☐	46-54/
prior military experience?	☐☐☐☐	☐☐☐☐	☐	55-63/

7. Does your agency give any credit toward seniority of position, compensation, or retirement for:

	No	Yes	
prior civilian law enforcement experience?.........	1 ☐	2 ☐	64/
prior military experience?....................................	1 ☐	2 ☐	65/

8. How many of the officers hired in 2006 and 2007 successfully graduated from the Academy? *Calendar or fiscal year reporting OK.*

	2006	2007
Number successfully completing the Academy	☐☐☐☐	☐☐☐☐

66-73/

CARD 01

4

CARD 02   5-6/
1-4/

9. **How many of the officers who completed the Academy in 2006 and 2007 (those listed in #8) also successfully completed the probation period post-Academy?** *Calendar or fiscal year reporting OK.*

	2006	2007
Number successfully completing the probation period post-Academy ……………………..……..	☐☐☐	☐☐☐

7-14/

10. **Please fill in the number of officers hired during 2006 and 2007 that fell into the following race and sex categories.**

2006		2007		
a. White Male ………….	☐☐☐	a.	White Male	☐☐☐ 15-20/
b. White Female ……….	☐☐☐	b.	White Female	☐☐☐ 21-26/
c. Other Male ………….	☐☐☐	c.	Other Male	☐☐☐ 27-32/
d. Other Female ……….	☐☐☐	d.	Other Female	☐☐☐ 33-38/

11. **Please fill in the number of officers hired during 2006 and 2007 that fell into the following educational categories.**

	High School Diploma or Equivalency	Some College (less than 120 credit hours)	120+ credit hours or College Graduate
a. 2006 ………….	☐☐☐	☐☐☐	☐☐☐ 39-47/
b. 2007 ………….	☐☐☐	☐☐☐	☐☐☐ 48-56/

CARD 02

5

12. To what extent did the following factors create difficulty in filling your agency's vacancies in 2007?

(Mark One Box Per Row)

	No Difficulty	Some Difficulty	Much Difficulty	N/A	
a. Amount of time between application and offer of employment...	₁☐	₂☐	₃☐	₄☐	57/
b.. Lack of qualified applicants	₁☐	₂☐	₃☐	₄☐	58/
c. Recruits failing to successfully complete training ...	₁☐	₂☐	₃☐	₄☐	59/
d. Level of entry pay	₁☐	₂☐	₃☐	₄☐	60/
e. Benefits package	₁☐	₂☐	₃☐	₄☐	61/
f. Current image in the community of police and/or the department	₁☐	₂☐	₃☐	₄☐	62/

RECRUITMENT STRATEGIES

13. Please mark all the recruiting methods or tools that your agency and/or the agency that assists with your recruitment used during 2007.

(Mark All That Apply)

₁☐ Newspaper   63/

₂☐ Magazines/Journals   64/

₃☐ Radio   65/

₄☐ Television   66/

₅☐ Internet   67/

₆☐ Billboards   68/

₇☐ Posters   69/

₈☐ Mass Mailings   70/

₉☐ Career Fairs   71/

₁₀☐ Community Organizations   72-73/

₁₁☐ High School outreach   74-75/

₁₂☐ Explorer and/or Cadets Program   76-77/

₁₃☐ College outreach   78-79/

₁₄☐ College Internships   80-81/

₁₅☐ Military Installations   82-83/

₁₆☐ Open House at the Police Department   84-85/

₁₇☐ Walk-in-Office   86-87/

₁₈☐ Other *(please specify)* _____ 88-90/

CARD 02

6

CARD 03   5-6/
1-4/

14. **Please mark any of the particular groups for which your agency and/or the agency that assists with your recruitment used targeted recruitment strategies during 2007:**

    (Mark All That Apply)

    ₁☐ Women   7/

    ₂☐ College graduates or those pursuing a higher education   8/

    ₃☐ People with previous police experience   9/

    ₄☐ People who speak a foreign language   10/

    ₅☐ Military veterans   11/

    ₆☐ Racial/ethnic minorities   12/

    ₇☐ Physically disabled   13/

    ₈☐ Other *(please specify)*_____   14-15/

    ₉☐ This department does not use any targeted recruitment strategies   16/

15. **Please fill in the number of applicants during 2006 and 2007 that fell into the following race and sex categories.** *By "applicant" we mean someone who has formally submitted an application.*

2006		2007	
a. White Male .... ☐☐☐	a.	White Male ☐☐☐	17-22/
b. White Female .... ☐☐☐	b.	White Female ☐☐☐	23-28/
c. Other Male .... ☐☐☐	c.	Other Male ☐☐☐	29-34/
d. Other Female .... ☐☐☐	d.	Other Female ☐☐☐	35-40/

16. **How many officers and/or civilians are assigned full-time to the recruitment process?**

    a. Officers   ☐☐☐   41-43/

    b. Civilians ☐☐☐   44-46/

17. **Does your police agency use a professional advertising agency for recruitment?**

    (Mark One)

    ₁☐ No   47/

    ₂☐ Yes

CARD 03

7

RECRUITMENT INCENTIVES

18. **Does your agency provide some type of award for those employees that refer successful applicants?**

    (Mark All That Apply)

    ₁☐ No   48/

    ₂☐ Yes, cash award → How much? $ ☐☐ , ☐☐☐   49-54/

    ₃☐ Yes, other: *(please specify)* _____   55-56/

19. **Which of the following incentives does your agency offer to recruits or officers?**

    19a. MONETARY INCENTIVES

    (Mark All That Apply)

    ₁☐ Employment or "signing" bonus .... $ ☐☐ , ☐☐☐   57-62/

    ₂☐ Paid a salary during recruit training.... $ ☐☐ . ☐☐ per hour   63-67/

    ₃☐ Academy graduation bonus .... $ ☐☐ , ☐☐☐   68-73/

    ₄☐ Relocation expenses   74/

    ₅☐ Housing stipend   75/

    ₆☐ Paid academy expenses   76/

    ₇☐ Other cash incentives .... $ ☐☐ , ☐☐☐   77-82/

    19b. EDUCATIONAL INCENTIVES

    (Mark All That Apply)

    ₁☐ Tuition for recruit training at an external academy/school   83/

    ₂☐ Reimbursement for college courses   84/

    ₃☐ Salary increases for college degrees   85/

    ₄☐ Schedule preferences for those taking college courses   86/

    19c. OTHER INCENTIVES

    (Mark All That Apply)

    ₁☐ Take-home car   87/

    ₂☐ Health club membership or reimbursement   88/

    ₃☐ Mortgage discount programs   89/

    ₄☐ Uniform allowance or uniforms provided by agency   90/

    ₅☐ Special pay rate by assignment (internal affairs, bomb squad, traffic, K-9, etc.)   91/

    ₆☐ Other incentives or bonuses: *(please specify)*_____   92-93/

    ₇☐ We do not offer any incentives or bonuses   94/

CARD 03

8

CARD 04   5-6/
          1-4/

COST OF RECRUITMENT

20. **Excluding personnel costs, what was the annual recruiting budget for your agency in 2006 and 2007? Please include all processes through acceptance of employment, including, but not limited to, outreach, advertising, applicant follow-up, and remedial support.**

    2006: $ [ ][ ][ ] , [ ][ ][ ]   7-12/

    2007: $ [ ][ ][ ] , [ ][ ][ ]   13-18/

RECRUITMENT STANDARDS

21. **Please indicate your agency's minimum education requirement for officer positions, if any.**

    (Mark One)

    1 ☐ Four-year college degree   19/

    2 ☐ Two-year college degree

    3 ☐ 46-60+ credit hours, no degree required

    4 ☐ 31-45 credit hours, no degree required

    5 ☐ 1-30 credit hours, no degree required

    6 ☐ High school diploma or equivalent

    7 ☐ No formal education requirement

22. **Please indicate any additional requirements your agency has for officer positions, if any.**

    (Mark All That Apply)

    1 ☐ U.S. citizen   20/

    2 ☐ Residency within your agency's service area   21/

    3 ☐ Driver's license holder   22/

    4 ☐ Able to pass vision test   23/

    5 ☐ Non-smoker   24/

    6 ☐ No dishonorable discharge from the armed services   25/

    7 ☐ Certified police academy graduate   26/

    8 ☐ Age range: Minimum [ ][ ]   Maximum [ ][ ]   27-31/

    9 ☐ Height restrictions   32/

    10 ☐ Weight restrictions   33-34/

    11 ☐ Physical agility test   35-36/

    12 ☐ Psychological test   37-38/

    13 ☐ Polygraph test   39-40/

    14 ☐ Medical test   41-42/

    15 ☐ Other: *(please specify)* _____   43-45/

    16 ☐ *No additional requirements for officer positions*   46-47/

                                                                          CARD 04

9

23. **Please indicate any items that could eliminate a person from receiving an offer of employment.**
    (Mark All That Apply)

    1 ☐ Any misdemeanor conviction — 48/
    2 ☐ Serious misdemeanor conviction — 49/
    3 ☐ Any felony arrest — 50/
    4 ☐ Any felony arrest in the past 2 years — 51/
    5 ☐ Any felony conviction — 52/
    6 ☐ Any prior drug use — 53/
    7 ☐ Any substance abuse arrest — 54/
    8 ☐ Any substance abuse arrest in the past 2 years — 55/
    9 ☐ Any substance abuse conviction — 56/
    10 ☐ Currently suspended drivers' license — 57-58/
    11 ☐ Excessive points on driving record in the past 2 years — 59-60/
    12 ☐ Poor credit score — 61-62/
    13 ☐ Termination from a law enforcement agency — 63-64/
    14 ☐ Other elimination criteria: *(please specify)*_____ — 65-67/

UNIONS

24. **Are officers within your agency covered by a collective bargaining agreement?**
    (Mark One)

    1 ☐ No — 68/
    2 ☐ Yes → **24a. What kind of collective bargaining agreement?**

      (Mark All That Apply)

      1 ☐ Working conditions — 69/
      2 ☐ Compensation — 70/
      3 ☐ Other — 71/

COMPENSATION

PAY AND BENEFITS

25. Enter the base annual pay (before deductions) sworn officers received in 2007 by the following rank positions.

	2007 Base annual pay (before deductions)		
a. Highest ranking uniformed officer	$ ____ , ____		7-12/
	Minimum	**Maximum**	
b. All ranks below the highest ranking uniformed officer but above Captain	$ ____ , ____	$ ____ , ____	13-24/
c. Captain or equivalent	$ ____ , ____	$ ____ , ____	25-36/
d. Lieutenant or equivalent	$ ____ , ____	$ ____ , ____	37-48/
e. Sergeant, First Line Supervisor or equivalent	$ ____ , ____	$ ____ , ____	49-60/
f. All ranks below Sergeant but above Officer	$ ____ , ____	$ ____ , ____	61-72/
g. Officer with 21 or more years of service	$ ____ , ____	$ ____ , ____	73-84/
h. Officer with 11-20 years of service	$ ____ , ____	$ ____ , ____	85-96/
i. Officer with 6-10 years of service	$ ____ , ____	$ ____ , ____	97-108/
j. Officer with 5 or less years of service	$ ____ , ____	$ ____ , ____	109-120/
k. Officer, newly hired	$ ____ , ____	$ ____ , ____	121-132/

CARD 06   5-6/
          1-4/

26.   Enter the typical number of hours worked by sworn officers in 2007 by the following rank positions.

	Typical Work Week	
	Average **Regular** Hours Worked	Average Compensated **Overtime** Hours Worked
a. Highest ranking uniformed officer			7-10/
b. All ranks below the highest ranking uniformed officer but above Captain			11-14/
c. Captain or equivalent			15-18/
d. Lieutenant or equivalent			19-22/
e. Sergeant, First Line Supervisor or equivalent			23-26/
f. All ranks below Sergeant but above Officer			27-30/
g. Officer with 21 or more years of service			31-34/
h. Officer with 11-20 years of service			35-38/
i. Officer with 6-10 years of service			39-42/
j. Officer with 5 or less years of service			43-46/
k. Officer, newly hired			47-50/

CARD 07

5-6/
1-4/

27. **Enter the total compensation (including base pay, special pay, overtime, etc.) sworn officers received in 2007 by the following rank positions.**

	2007 Total Compensation		
		Minimum	**Maximum**
a. Highest ranking uniformed officer	$ ☐☐☐ , ☐☐☐		7-12/
b. All ranks below the highest ranking uniformed officer but above Captain		$ ☐☐☐ , ☐☐☐	$ ☐☐☐ , ☐☐☐	13-24/
c. Captain or equivalent		$ ☐☐☐ , ☐☐☐	$ ☐☐☐ , ☐☐☐	25-36/
d. Lieutenant or equivalent		$ ☐☐☐ , ☐☐☐	$ ☐☐☐ , ☐☐☐	37-48/
e. Sergeant, First Line Supervisor or equivalent		$ ☐☐☐ , ☐☐☐	$ ☐☐☐ , ☐☐☐	49-60/
f. All ranks below Sergeant but above Officer		$ ☐☐☐ , ☐☐☐	$ ☐☐☐ , ☐☐☐	61-72/
g. Officer with 21 or more years of service		$ ☐☐☐ , ☐☐☐	$ ☐☐☐ , ☐☐☐	73-84/
h. Officer with 11-20 years of service		$ ☐☐☐ , ☐☐☐	$ ☐☐☐ , ☐☐☐	85-96/
i. Officer with 6-10 years of service		$ ☐☐☐ , ☐☐☐	$ ☐☐☐ , ☐☐☐	97-108/
j. Officer with 5 or less years of service		$ ☐☐☐ , ☐☐☐	$ ☐☐☐ , ☐☐☐	109-120/
k. Officer, newly hired		$ ☐☐☐ , ☐☐☐	$ ☐☐☐ , ☐☐☐	121-132/

CARD 08   5-6/
1-4/

28. What was your authorized force strength in each of the following rank positions at the beginning of 2007?

	Authorized Number of Officers	
a. Highest ranking uniformed officer		7-11/
b. All ranks below the highest ranking uniformed officer but above Captain		12-16/
c. Captain or equivalent		17-21/
d. Lieutenant or equivalent		22-26/
e. Sergeant, First Line Supervisor or equivalent		27-31/
f. All ranks below Sergeant but above Officer		32-36/
g. Officer		37-41/

29. How many total vacancies did you experience in each of the following categories at the beginning of 2007 (even if filled at some point during the year)?

	Number of Vacancies	
a. Highest ranking uniformed officer		42-46/
b. All ranks below the highest ranking uniformed officer but above Captain		47-51/
c. Captain or equivalent		52-56/
d. Lieutenant or equivalent		57-61/
e. Sergeant, First Line Supervisor or equivalent		62-66/
f. All ranks below Sergeant but above Officer		67-71/
g. Officer		72-76/

CARD 08

CARD 09   5-6/
1-4/

30. <u>During **2006**</u>, did your department change (raise, lower, adjust) compensation?

(Mark One)

₁ ☐ No → Skip to 31   7/

₂ ☐ Yes → **30a. What impact has this change had on compensation for <u>new recruits</u>?**

   (Mark One)

   ₁ ☐ Raised compensation   8/

   ₂ ☐ Lowered compensation

   ₃ ☐ No change in compensation

   30b. What impact has the above had on reaching your recruitment goals?

   (Mark One)

   ₁ ☐ Easier to meet recruitment goals   9/

   ₂ ☐ No impact on recruitment

   ₃ ☐ More difficult to meet recruitment goals

31. **Does your agency allow officers to work secondary or other employment?**

(Mark One)

₁ ☐ No → Skip to 32   10/

₂ ☐ Yes → **31a. What limit, if any, does your agency place on the maximum number of hours an officer can work at a second job or other employment?**

   (Mark One)

   ₁ ☐ No limit   11-13/

   ₂ ☐ Hours per week   ☐☐

   ₃ ☐ Hours per day   ☐☐

   ₄ ☐ Other: *(please specify)* _____

   31b. For outside employment (a.k.a., details):
   Is this work centrally assigned, or assigned by the local area command (precinct, district, etc.)?

   (Mark All That Apply)

   ₁ ☐ Centrally assigned   14/

   ₂ ☐ Assigned by the local area command (precinct, district, etc.)   15/

   ₃ ☐ Other   16/

POSSIBILITIES FOR PROMOTION

32. **What is the minimum number of years that an officer must serve before being eligible for the department's lowest supervisory rank position?**

    ☐☐ Years   17-18/

33. **How are promotion exams scheduled for the first supervisory rank position?**

    (Mark One)

    1 ☐ Based on vacancies   19-21/

    2 ☐ Based on a set calendar → Once every ☐☐ month / year. *Circle One.*

    3 ☐ When current lists expire

    4 ☐ Other *(please specify)* _____

34. **Is there a minimum number of years someone must serve in that grade before being promoted to the next supervisory position?**

    1 ☐ No → Skip to 35   22/

    2 ☐ Yes → **34a. What is the minimum number of years a person must serve in that grade before being promoted to the next supervisory position?**

    ☐☐ Years   23-24/

35. **How are promotion exams scheduled for the next supervisory position?**

    (Mark One)

    1 ☐ Based on vacancies   25-28/

    2 ☐ Based on a set calendar → Once every ☐☐ month / year. *Circle One*

    3 ☐ When current lists expire

    4 ☐ Other *(please specify)* _____

CARD 09

16

RETIREMENT

36. **Does your agency have a mandatory retirement age for officers?**

    (Mark One)

    ₁☐ No   *29-31/*

    ₂☐ Yes → What is that age? ☐☐ years old

37. **Please provide information on your agency's retirement plan.**

    a. Minimum years of service for full vesting in retirement plan .... ☐☐ years   *32-33/*

    b. Required years of service for immediate full retirement .... ☐☐ years   *34-35/*

    c. Minimum age for immediate full retirement .... ☐☐ years old   *36-37/*

    d. % of base pay in first eligible year of full retirement .... ☐☐☐ . ☐ %   *38-41/*

    e. Other system *(please describe)* _____   *42/*

38. **Is your agency's retirement plan a local system (municipal, city, county, etc.), a state system, a combination of both, or something else?**

    (Mark One)

    ₁☐ Local system   *43-44/*

    ₂☐ State system

    ₃☐ Combination of local system and state system

    ₄☐ Other: *(please specify)* _____

39. **Does your agency offer any kind of incentive program to encourage officers to delay retirement (for example, a DROP program)?**

    (Mark One)

    ₁☐ No   *45/*

    ₂☐ Yes

DEPARTMENTAL STATISTICS

This section will ask detailed questions about your department's personnel profile and may require close examination and analysis of your personnel records and databases. We are aware that compiling it will be burdensome but the level of detail we request is absolutely critical to ensure we have the specific information necessary to develop concrete, data-driven recruitment and retention lessons for the law enforcement community.

For questions 40 and 43 we need information on the personnel profile and attrition by years on the force and rank. We would like to make providing this information as simple and efficient as possible for you. In so doing, you may provide this information via the method most convenient for you:

- You may complete the tables provided in questions 40 and 43.
- You may provide a "flat-file" or spreadsheet that provides this detail for every officer on the force (question 40) and every officer who left the force (question 43). Please do not provide any personally identifiable information (e.g., Social Security Numbers.) NOTE: We can work with you on de-identifying your data as needed. You may provide this information either electronically (preferred) or in paper form (email PDRR@rand.org to arrange transmittal).
- You may provide a "flat-file" or spreadsheet in any other format (e.g., data runs by rank and year of hire or runs by rank and years on the force) that will allow us to calculate the number of officers within each rank by years on the force (question 40) and the number of officers who left the force within each rank by years on the force (question 43). You may provide this information either electronically (preferred) or in paper form (email PDRR@rand.org to arrange transmittal). As above, we ask that you do not provide any personally identifiable data. However, we can work with you on de-identifying your data if necessary.
- If you have this information in another form that is more convenient for you to present, please email us at PDRR@rand.org and we will work with you to accommodate your format.

Please remember to complete questions 41 and 42 even if you are sending a flat file or spreadsheet in response to questions 40 and 43.

CARD 10   5-6/
           1-4/

40. Please complete the following workforce by years of continuous service and rank chart on the date of June 30, 2007. Fill in the number of officers for each rank position according to their years of continuous service.

For example, if on June 30, 2007 your agency had three captains, two of which had 6-10 years of continuous service and one of which had 15, in the "captain or equivalent" column you would place a "2" in the row corresponding to 10 years of continuous service and a "1" in the row corresponding to 11-15 years of continuous service. The same method applies to all of the ranks.

Years of Continuous Service	RANK							
	Highest ranking uniformed officer	All ranks below highest ranking uniformed officer but above Captain	Captain or Equivalent	Lieutenant or Equivalent	Sergeant, First Line Supervisor, or Equivalent	All ranks below Sergeant but above Officer	Officer	
1 or less	☐	☐	☐	☐	☐	☐	☐	7-25/
2-5	☐	☐	☐	☐	☐	☐	☐	26-44/
6-10	☐	☐	☐	☐	☐	☐	☐	45-63/
11-15	☐	☐	☐	☐	☐	☐	☐	64-82/
16-20	☐	☐	☐	☐	☐	☐	☐	83-101/
21-25	☐	☐	☐	☐	☐	☐	☐	102-120/
26-30	☐	☐	☐	☐	☐	☐	☐	121-139/
30 or more	☐	☐	☐	☐	☐	☐	☐	140-158/

CARD 11   5-6/
           1-4/

41. Please complete the following chart by filling in the number of officers in your department as of June 30, 2006 and June 30, 3007 by race/ethnicity, divided out by gender.

Year	As of June 30, 2006		As of June 30, 2007		
Gender	Male	Female	Male	Female	
RACE/ETHNICITY					
White, not of Hispanic origin	☐	☐	☐	☐	7-26/
Black, not of Hispanic origin	☐	☐	☐	☐	27-46/
Hispanic origin, any race	☐	☐	☐	☐	47-66/
Other	☐	☐	☐	☐	67-86/

CARD 10/CARD 11

CARD 12   5-6/
           1-4/

42.   Please complete the following chart of your agency's <u>authorized (budgeted) and actual strength</u> for full-time officers and full-time civilian employees as of June 30, 2006 and June 30, 2007.

Officers	As of June 30, 2006	As of June 30, 2007	
a. Authorized Strength	☐☐ , ☐☐☐	☐☐ , ☐☐☐	7-16/
b. Actual Strength	☐☐ , ☐☐☐	☐☐ , ☐☐☐	17-26/

Civilians	As of June 30, 2006	As of June 30, 2007	
c. Authorized Strength	☐☐ , ☐☐☐	☐☐ , ☐☐☐	27-36/
d. Actual Strength	☐☐ , ☐☐☐	☐☐ , ☐☐☐	37-46/

CARD 13   5-6/
           1-4/

ATTRITION

43.   Please complete the following attrition by years of continuous service and rank chart for 2007. Fill in the number of officers who left your agency for each rank position according to their years of continuous service.

For example, if in 2007 two lieutenants separated from your agency, one of which had 6-10 years of continuous service and one of which had 12, in the "lieutenant or equivalent" column you would place a "1" in the row corresponding to 8 years of continuous service and a "1" in the row corresponding to 11-15 years of continuous service. The same method applies to all of the ranks.

Years of Continuous Service	RANK							
	Highest ranking uniformed officer	All ranks below highest ranking uniformed officer but above Captain	Captain or Equivalent	Lieutenant or Equivalent	Sergeant, First Line Supervisor, or Equivalent	All ranks below Sergeant but above Officer	Officer	
1 or less	☐	☐☐☐	☐☐☐	☐☐☐	☐☐☐	☐☐☐	☐☐☐	7-25/
2-5	☐	☐☐☐	☐☐☐	☐☐☐	☐☐☐	☐☐☐	☐☐☐	26-44/
6-10	☐	☐☐☐	☐☐☐	☐☐☐	☐☐☐	☐☐☐	☐☐☐	45-63/
11-15	☐	☐☐☐	☐☐☐	☐☐☐	☐☐☐	☐☐☐	☐☐☐	64-82/
16-20	☐	☐☐☐	☐☐☐	☐☐☐	☐☐☐	☐☐☐	☐☐☐	83-101/
21-25	☐	☐☐☐	☐☐☐	☐☐☐	☐☐☐	☐☐☐	☐☐☐	102-120/
26-30	☐	☐☐☐	☐☐☐	☐☐☐	☐☐☐	☐☐☐	☐☐☐	121-139/
30 or more	☐	☐☐☐	☐☐☐	☐☐☐	☐☐☐	☐☐☐	☐☐☐	140-158/

CARD 12/CARD 13

20

CARD 14

5-6/
1-4/

44. Enter your agency's budget for personnel for fiscal year 2006.

$ [ ][ ] , [ ][ ][ ] , [ ][ ][ ] , [ ][ ][ ]

7-17/

45. **Enter your agency's operating budget for FY06 not including personnel.** If data are not available, please provide an estimate. Do not include building construction costs or major equipment purchases.

$ [ ][ ] , [ ][ ][ ] , [ ][ ][ ] , [ ][ ][ ]

18-28/

CONTACT INFORMATION

Person to contact regarding this report:

Name

[ ]

Title

[ ]

Police Department

[ ]

Phone

Ext.

([ ][ ][ ]) [ ][ ][ ] — [ ][ ][ ][ ]   [ ][ ][ ][ ][ ][ ]

Fax

([ ][ ][ ]) [ ][ ][ ] — [ ][ ][ ][ ]

Email address

[ ]

CARD 14

21

THIS PAGE INTENTIONALLY BLANK

22

THIS PAGE INTENTIONALLY BLANK

23

References

Alpert, Geoffrey P., "Hiring and Promoting Police Officers in Small Departments: The Role of Psychological Testing," *Criminal Law Bulletin*, Vol. 27, No. 3, May/June 1991, pp. 261–269.

Archbold, C. A., and E. R. Maguire, "Studying Civil Suits Against the Police: A Serendipitous Findings of Sample Selection Bias," *Police Quarterly,* Vol. 5, 2002, pp. 222–249.

Armstrong, Kristen, "Arlington's Police Force Makes It to Full Staffing," *Sun Gazette Newpapers*, November 15, 2006.

Birati, Assa, and Aharon Tziner, "Successful Promotion of Early Retirement: A Quantitative Approach," *Human Resource Management Review,* Vol. 5, No. 1, Spring 1995, pp. 53–62.

Bowyer, Richard F., "Recruiting 21st Century Army Warriors: A Task Requiring National Attention," U.S. Army War College Strategy Research Project, Carlisle, Pa.: U.S. Army War College, 2007.

Braga, Anthony A., "The Effects of Hot Spots Policing on Crime," *The Annals of the American Academy of Political and Social Science*, Vol. 578, 2001, pp. 104–125.

Clarke, R. V., and H. Goldstein, "Reducing Theft at Construction Sites: Lessons from a Problem-Oriented Project," in N. Tilley, ed., *Analysis for Crime Prevention*, *Crime Prevention Studies*, Vol. 13, Monsey, N.Y.: Criminal Justice Press, 2002.

Clear, T. R., and N. A. Frost, "Informing Public Policy," *Criminology & Public Policy*, Vol. 6, 2007, pp. 633–640.

Cooper, Christine, and Samantha Ingram, "Retaining Officers in the Police Service: A Study of Resignations and Transfers in Ten Forces," London: Home Office Communication Development Unit, NCJ 205347, 2004. As of May 28, 2010:
http://www.homeoffice.gov.uk/rds/pdfs04/r212.pdf

COPS Office, *Community Policing Dispatch*, Washington, D.C.: U.S. Department of Justice, Office of Community-Oriented Policing Services, June 2009. As of July 7, 2009:
http://www.cops.usdoj.gov/html/dispatch/June_2009/hiring_recovery.htm

Davidson, R., and J. G. MacKinnon, *Estimation and Inference in Econometrics*, New York: Oxford University Press, 1993.

Davis, Lois M., Louis T. Mariano, Jennifer E. Pace, Sarah K. Cotton, and Paul Steinberg, *Combating Terrorism: How Prepared Are State and Local Response Organizations?* Santa Monica, Calif.: RAND Corporation, MG-309-OSD, 2006. As of March 27, 2010:
http://www.rand.org/pubs/monographs/MG309/

Davis, Lois M., K. Jack Riley, Greg Ridgeway, Jennifer Pace, Sarah K. Cotton, Paul S. Steinberg, Kelly Damphousse, and Brent L. Smith, *When Terrorism Hits Home: How Prepared Are State and Local Law Enforcement?* Santa Monica, Calif.: RAND Corporation, MG-104, 2004. As of March 27, 2010:
http://www.rand.org/pubs/monographs/MG104/

DeRugy, Veronique, "What Does Homeland Security Spending Buy?" Washington, D.C.: American Enterprise Institute for Public Policy Research, Working Paper #18213, December 14, 2006. As of October 11, 2009:
http://www.aei.org/docLib/20061214_FactsandFigures.pdf

Draut, Tamara, "Economic State of Young America," New York, N.Y.: Demos, Spring, 2008. As of October 18, 2009:
http://www.demos.org/pubs/esya_web.pdf

Draut, Tamara, and Javier Silva, "Generation Broke: Borrowing to Make Ends Meet," New York: Demos, Briefing Paper #2, October 2004. As of October 11, 2009:
http://archive.demos.org/pubs/Generation_Broke.pdf

Eck, J. E., and W. Spelman, "Who Ya Gonna Call? The Police as Problem Busters," *Crime and Delinquency*, Vol. 33, 1987, pp. 31–52.

Eckstein, Zvi, and Kenneth I. Wolpin, "The Specification and Estimation of Dynamic Stochastic Discrete Choice Models: A Survey," *The Journal of Human Resources*, Vol. 24, No. 4, Autumn 1989, pp. 562–598.

Egan, Timothy, "Police Forces, Their Ranks Thin, Offer Bonuses, Bounties and More," *New York Times*, December 28, 2005. As of June 24, 2010:
http://www.nytimes.com/2005/12/28/national/28police.html

Fechter, Alan E., "Impact of Pay and Draft Policy on Army Enlistment Behavior," in Gates Commission, ed., *Studies Prepared for the President's Commission on an All-Volunteer Armed Force*, Washington, D.C.: U.S. Government Printing Office, 1970, pp. II-3-1 to II-3-59.

Frawley, Kathleen E., *The Effects of 9/11 on the Fire Fighter Labor Market*, Bloomington, Ill.: Illinois Wesleyan University, Economics Department Honors Projects paper 7, 2006. As of June 24, 2010:
http://digitalcommons.iwu.edu/econ_honproj/7/

Frost, J. A., "Predictors of Job Satisfaction and Turnover Intention in Police Organizations: A Procedural Approach," Chicago: The University of Chicago, Ph.D. dissertation, 2006.

Fyfe, James J., "Too Many Missing Cases: Holes in Our Knowledge About Police Use of Force," *Justice Research and Policy*, Vol. 4, 2002, pp. 87–102.

Fyfe, James J., Jack R. Greene, William F. Walsh, O. W. Wilson, and Roy McLaren, *Police Administration*, 5th Edition, New York: McGraw Hill, 1997.

"Getting Out of Dodge: Young Cops in Far Rockaway Recite the NYUPD Blues and Try to Flee to Suburban Jobs," *Village Voice*, January 29, 2008. As of March 30, 2010:
http://www.villagevoice.com/2008-01-29/news/getting-out-of-dodge/

Gilmore Commission, "Forging America's New Normalcy: Securing Our Homeland, Preserving Our Liberty," *The Fifth Annual Report to the President and the Congress of the Advisory Panel to Assess Domestic Response Capabilities for Terrorism Involving Weapons of Mass Destruction*, 2003. As of March 27, 2010:
http://www.rand.org/nsrd/terrpanel/volume_v/volume_v.pdf

Goldstein, Herman, *Policing a Free Society*, Cambridge, Mass.: Ballinger Publishing, 1977.

Gordon, Roger H., and Alan S. Blinder, "Market Wages, Reservation Wages, and Retirement Decisions," *Journal of Public Economics*, Vol. 14, No. 12, October 1980, pp. 277–308.

Gottfredson, Michael R., and Don M. Gottfredson, *Decision Making in Criminal Justice: Toward the Rational Exercise of Discretion*, Second Edition, New York: Plenum Press, 1988.

Greene, William H., *Econometric Analysis*, 4th Edition, Upper Saddle River, N.J.: Prentice Hall, 2000.

Grissmer, David W., and Bernard D. Rostker, "Military Manpower in a Changing World," in Joseph Kruzel, ed., *American Defense Annual: 1991–1992*, New York: Lexington Books, 1992, pp. 127–145.

Gujarati, Damodar N., *Basic Econometrics*, 4th Edition,, New York: McGraw-Hill, 2003.

Hayes, Hennessey, and Kathleen Daly, "Youth Justice Conferencing and Reoffending," *Justice Quarterly*, Vol. 20, No. 4, December 2003, pp. 725–764.

Hickman, Matthew J., and Brian A. Reaves, "Local Police Departments, 2003," Washington, D.C.: U.S. Department of Justice, Office of Justice Programs, Bureau of Justice Statistics, NCJ 210118, 2006. As of July 14, 2009: http://www.ojp.usdoj.gov/bjs/pub/pdf/lpd03.pdf

Hogue, Mark C., Tommie Black, and Robert T. Sigler, "The Differential Use of Screening Techniques in the Recruitment of Police Officers," *American Journal of Police,* Vol. 13, No. 2, 1994, pp. 113–124.

Holtom, Brooks C., Terence R. Mitchell, Thomas W. Lee, and Marion B. Eberly, "Turnover and Retention Research: A Glance At the Past, A Closer View of the Present, and a Venture into the Future," *The Academy of Management Annals,* Vol. 2, No. 1, 2008, pp. 231–274.

Johnston, Lloyd D., Patrick M. O'Malley, Jerald G. Bachman, and John E. Schulenberg, "Various Stimulant Drugs Show Continuing Gradual Declines Among Teens in 2008, Most Illicit Drugs Hold Steady," Ann Arbor, Mich.: University of Michigan News Service, December 11, 2008. As of November 20, 2009: http://monitoringthefuture.org/data/08data.html#2008data-drugs

Jordan, William T., Lorie Fridell, Donald Faggiani, and Bruce Kubu, "Attracting Females and Racial/Ethnic Minorities to Law Enforcement," *Journal of Criminal Justice,* Vol. 37, No. 4, July–August 2009, pp. 333–341.

Kane, Tim, "The Demographics of Military Enlistment After 9/11," Washington, D.C.: The Heritage Foundation, Executive Memorandum #987, November 3, 2005. As of November 11, 2009: http://www.heritage.org/research/nationalsecurity/em987.cfm

Kennedy, D. M., A. A. Braga, A. M. Piehl, and E. J. Waring, *Reducing Gun Violence: The Boston Gun Project's Operation Ceasefire,* Washington, D.C.: U.S. Department of Justice, 2001.

Kondrasuk, Jack N., "The Effects of 9/11 on Human Resource Management: Recovery, Reconsideration, and Renewal," *Employee Responsibilities and Rights Journal,* Vol. 16, No. 1, March 2004, pp. 25–35.

Koper, C. S., E. R. Maguire, and G. E. Moore, *Hiring and Retention Issues in Police Agencies: Readings on the Determinants of Police Strength, Hiring and Retention of Officers, and the Federal COPS Program,* Washington, D.C.: Urban Institute Justice Policy Center, NCJRS No. 193428, 2002.

Langworthy, R. H., "LEMAS: A Comparative Organizational Research Platform," *Justice Research and Policy,* Vol. 4, 2002, pp. 21–38.

Lipsey, M. W., *Design Sensitivity: Statistical Power for Experimental Research,* Thousand Oaks, Calif.: Sage Publications, 1990.

Lynch, Jessica E., and Michelle Tuckey, "Understanding Voluntary Turnover: An Examination of Resignations in Australasian Police Organizations," Payneham, Australia: Australasian Centre for Policing Research, 2004.

Maguire, E. R., *Police Departments as Learning Laboratories*, Police Foundation: Ideas in American Policing, No. 6, 2004.

Maguire, Edward R., and William R. King, "Trends in the Policing Industry," *The Annals of the American Academy of Political and Social Science*, Vol. 593, 2004, pp. 15–41.

Maguire, Edward R., and Stephen D. Mastrofski, "Patterns of Community Policing in the United States," *Police Quarterly*, Vol. 3, No. 1, March 2000, pp. 4–45.

Maguire, E. R., and R. Schulte-Murray, "Issues and Patterns in the Comparative International Study of Police Strength," *International Journal of Comparative Sociology*, Vol. 42, 2001, pp. 75–100.

Maguire, E. R., J. B. Snipes, C. D. Uchida, and M. Townsend, "Counting Cops: Estimating the Number of Police Departments and Police Officers in the USA," *Policing: An International Journal of Police Strategies & Management*, Vol. 21, 1998, pp. 97–120.

Makinen, Gail, *The Economic Effects of 9/11: A Retrospective Assessment*, Washington, D.C.: Congressional Research Service, September 27, 2002. As of November 11, 2009:
http://www.fas.org/irp/crs/RL31617.pdf

Manolatos, Tony, "S.D. Cops Flee City's Fiscal Mess, Seek Jobs at Other Departments," *San Diego Union-Tribune*, July 5, 2006. As of November 11, 2009:
http://sports.uniontrib.com/uniontrib/20060705/news_1n5gary.html

Martin, S. E., *Breaking and Entering: Policewomen on Patrol,* Berkeley: University of California Press, 1980.

McGarrell, Edmund. F., and Natalie K Hipple,, "Family Group Conferencing and Re-Offending Among First-Time Juvenile Offenders: The Indianapolis Experiment," *Justice Quarterly*, Vol. 24, No. 2, June 2007, pp. 221–246.

McGarrell, E. F., S. Chermak, and A. Weiss, "Reducing Gun Violence: Evaluation of the Indianapolis Police Department's Directed Patrol Project," Washington, D.C.: National Institute of Justice, Special Report, 2002. As of July 22, 2010:
http://www.ncjrs.gov/txtfiles1/nij/188740.txt

McGarrell, E. F., S. Chermak, A. Weiss, and J. M. Wilson, "Reducing Firearms Violence Through Directed Patrol," *Criminology & Public Policy,* Vol. 1, 2001, pp. 119–148.

Merck, J. W., and Kathleen Hall, *A Markovian Flow Model: The Analysis of Movement in Large-Scale (Military) Personnel Systems*, Santa Monica, Calif.: RAND Corporation, R-514-PR, February 1971. As of March 30, 2010: http://www.rand.org/pubs/reports/R0514/

Mobley, William H., *Employee Turnover: Causes, Consequences, and Control*, Reading, Mass.: Addison-Wesley, 1982.

National Research Council, Committee on the Youth Population and Military Recruitment, *Attitudes, Aptitudes, and Aspirations of American Youth: Implications for Military Recruiting*, 2003. As of November 20, 2009: http://www.nap.edu/catalog.php?record_id=10478

New South Wales Council on the Cost of Government (NSWCCG), *First Report*, Sydney, Australia, 1996.

Orrick, W. Dwayne, "Maximizing Officer Retention," Presentation at the RAND Summit on Recruitment and Retention, Washington, D.C., June 2008a. As of September 2, 2009: http://www.cops.usdoj.gov/Default.asp?Item=2101

Orrick, W. Dwayne, *Recruitment, Retention, and Turnover of Police Personnel: Reliable, Practical, and Effective Solutions*, Springfield, Ill.: Charles C. Thomas Publishers, 2008b.

Pomfret, John, "Police Finding It Hard to Fill Jobs," *Washington Post*, March 27, 2006. As of June 24, 2010: http://www.washingtonpost.com/wp-dyn/content/article/2006/03/26/AR2006032600995.html

Proffer, Ben, "More Money, More NYPD Recruits," *New York*, July 6, 2008. As of March 30, 2009: http://nymag.com/news/intelligencer/48332/

Raganella, A. J., and M. D. White, "Race, Gender, and Motivation for Becoming a Police Officer: Implications for Building a Representative Police Department," *Journal of Criminal Justice*, Vol. 32, 2004, pp. 501–513.

Raymond, Barbara, Laura J. Hickman, Laura Miller, and Jennifer S. Wong, *Police Personnel Challenges After September 11: Anticipating Expanded Duties and a Changing Labor Pool*, Santa Monica, Calif.: RAND Corporation, OP-154-RC, 2005. As of May 5, 2009: http://www.rand.org/pubs/occasional_papers/OP154/

Riley, K. Jack, Gregory F. Treverton, Jeremy M. Wilson, and Lois M. Davis, *State and Local Intelligence in the War on Terrorism*, Santa Monica, Calif.: RAND Corporation, MG-394-RC, 2005. As of March 27, 2010: http://www.rand.org/pubs/monographs/MG394/

Rostker, Bernard, *I Want You! The Evolution of the All-Volunteer Force*, Santa Monica, Calif.: RAND Corporation, MG-265-RC, 2006. As of July 21, 2010: http://www.rand.org/pubs/monographs/MG265/

Rostker, Bernard, William M. Hix, and Jeremy M. Wilson, *Recruitment and Retention: Lessons for the New Orleans Police Department,* Santa Monica, CA: RAND Corporation, MG-585-RC, 2007. As of March 27, 2010: http://www.rand.org/pubs/monographs/MG585/

Scrivner, Ellen, *Innovations in Police Recruitment and Hiring: Hiring in the Spirit of Service*, Washington, D.C.: Office of Community Oriented Policing Services, 2006. As of May 5, 2009: http://www.cops.usdoj.gov/RIC/ResourceDetail.aspx?RID=113

Sherman, L. W., and B. D. Glick, "The Quality of Police Arrest Statistics," *Police Foundation Reports,* Washington, D.C.: Police Foundation, 1984.

Sherman, Lawrence, and Heather Strang, "Restorative Justice: What We Know and How We Know It," *Jerry Lee Program on Randomized Controlled Trials in Restorative Justice, Working Paper #1*, Philadelphia: University of Pennsylvania, Jerry Lee Center of Criminology, 2004.

Sherman, Lawrence, Heather Strang, and Daniel Woods, *Recidivism Patterns in the Canberra Reintegrative Shaming Experiments (RISE)*, Canberra: Centre for Restorative Justice, Australian National University, 2000.

Slater, Harold R., and Martin Reiser, "A Comparative Study of Factors Influencing Police Recruitment," *Journal of Police Science and Administration,* Vol. 16, No. 3, 1988, pp. 168–176.

Smith, A. R., "Defense Manpower Studies," *Operations Research Quarterly,* Vol. 19, No. 3, September 1968.

Spielman, Fran, "Early Retirement for Cops Helps Budget, Not Force," *Chicago Sun-Times*, July 23, 2009. As of October 12, 2009: http://www.suntimes.com/news/cityhall/1681991,chicago-cops-shortage-retirement-072309.article

Stone, V., and R. Tuffin, "Attitudes of People from Minority Ethnic Communities Towards a Career in the Police Service," *Home Office Police Research Series Paper, 136,* London: Home Office, 2000. As of July 17, 2010: http://rds.homeoffice.gov.uk/rds/prgpdfs/prs136.pdf

Sturm, R., J. S. Ringel, D. Lakdawalla, J. Bhattacharya, D. P. Goldman, M. D. Hurd, G. Joyce, C. W. A. Panis, and T. Andreyeva, *Obesity and Disability: The Shape of Things to Come*, Santa Monica, Calif.: RAND Corporation, RB-9043, 2004. As of November 11, 2009: http://www.rand.org/pubs/research_briefs/RB9043-1/

Switzer, Merlin E., *Recruitment and Retention: Best Practices Update*, Sacramento, Calif.: Commission on Peace Officer Standards and Training, April 2006.

Taylor, Bruce, Bruce Kubu, Lorie Fridell, Carter Rees, Tom Jordan, and Jason Cheney, *Cop Crunch: Identifying Strategies for Dealing with the Recruiting and Hiring Crisis in Law Enforcement*, Washington, D.C.: Police Executive Research Forum, 2006. As of November 11, 2009:
http://www.ncjrs.gov/pdffiles1/nij/grants/213800.pdf

Tulgan, Bruce, *Managing Generation X: How to Bring Out the Best in Young Talent*, Oxford: Capstone, 2000.

Twenge, Jean M., and Stacy M. Campbell, "Generational Differences in Psychological Traits and Their Impact on the Workplace," *Journal of Managerial Psychology*, Vol. 23, No. 8, 2008, pp. 862–877.

Uchida, C. D., C. Bridgeforth, and C. F. Wellford, "Law Enforcement Statistics: The State of the Art," *American Journal of Police,* Vol. 5, 1986, pp. 23–43.

Uchida, Craig D., and William R. King, "Police Employee Data: Elements and Validity," *Justice Research and Policy,* Vol. 4, 2002, pp. 11–19.

U.S. Bureau of Labor Statistics, "May 2008 National Occupational Employment and Wage Estimates, United States," Occupational Employment Statistics, last modified May 29, 2009. As of June 24, 2010:
http://www.bls.gov/oes/2008/may/oes_nat.htm

U.S. Department of Defense, Office of the Undersecretary of Defense, Personnel, and Readiness, "Population Representation in the Military Services: Trends in Propensity," Washington, D.C.: Department of Defense, March 2003.

U.S. Department of Justice, Bureau of Justice Statistics, Law Enforcement Management and Administrative Statistics (LEMAS): 2003 Sample Survey of Law Enforcement Agencies, ICPSR04411-v1, Washington, D.C.: U.S. Department of Commerce, Bureau of the Census (producer), Ann Arbor, Mich.: Inter-University Consortium for Political and Social Research (distributor), doi:10.3886/ICPSR04411, 2006. As of August 30, 2010:
http://www.icpsr.umich.edu/cocoon/NACJD/STUDY/04411.xml

Van Maanen, J., "Observations on the Making of Policemen," *Human Organization,* Vol. 32, 1973, pp. 407–418.

Walker, Samuel, ed., *Records of the Wickersham Commission on Law Observance and Enforcement*, Bethesda, Md.: University Publications of America, 1997. As of November 11, 2009:
http://www.lexisnexis.com/documents/academic/upa_cis/1965_WickershamCommPt1.pdf

Walker, Samuel, *Police Accountability: Current Issues and Research Needs*, Washington, D.C.: U.S. Department of Justice, NCJ 218583, November 2006.

Wheeler, Christopher H., "Local Market Scale and the Pattern of Job Changes Among Young Men," *Regional Science & Urban Economics*, Vol. 38, No. 2, March 2008, pp. 101–118.

White, H., "A Heteroscedasticity Consistent Covariance Matrix Estimator and a Direct Test of Heteroscedasticity," *Econometrica,* Vol. 48, 1980, pp. 817–818.

White, Michael D., and Gipsy Escobar, "Making Good Cops in the Twenty-First Century: Emerging Issues for the Effective Recruitment, Selection and Training of Police in the United States and Abroad," *Crime and Criminal Justice*, Vol. 22, No. 1-2, March 2008, pp. 119–134.

Wilson, Jeremy M., *Community Policing in America*, New York: Routledge, 2006.

Wilson, Jeremy M., and Amy G. Cox, *Community Policing and Crime: The Process and Impact of Problem-Solving in Oakland,* Santa Monica, Calif.: RAND Corporation, TR-635-BPA, 2008. As of March 27, 2010:
http://www.rand.org/pubs/technical_reports/TR635/

Wilson, Jeremy M., Amy G. Cox, Tommy L. Smith, Hans Bos, and Terry Fain, *Community Policing and Violence Prevention in Oakland: Measure Y in Action,* Santa Monica, Calif.: RAND Corporation, TR-546-BPA, 2007. As of March 27, 2010:
http://www.rand.org/pubs/technical_reports/TR546/

Wilson, Jeremy M., Erin Dalton, Charles Scheer, and Clifford A. Grammich, *Police Recruitment and Retention for the New Millennium: The State of Knowledge*, Santa Monica, Calif.: RAND Corporation, MG-959-DOJ, forthcoming.

Wilson, Jeremy M., and Clifford A. Grammich, *Police Recruitment and Retention in the Contemporary Urban Environment: A National Discussion of Personnel Experiences and Promising Practices from the Front Lines*, Santa Monica, Calif: RAND Corporation, CF-261-DOJ, 2009. As of March 27, 2010:
http://www.rand.org/pubs/conf_proceedings/CF261/

Wilson, Jeremy M., Bernie Rostker, and Mike Hix, "Police Recruitment and Retention in New Orleans: Crisis as Catalyst," presentation at the RAND Summit on Recruitment and Retention, Washington, D.C., June 2008. As of September 2, 2009:
http://www.cops.usdoj.gov/pdf/conference/rand/WilsonPoliceRecruitmentNO.pdf

Wilson, Michael J., "Youth Attitude Tracking Study: 1999 Propensity and Advertising Report," Arlington, Va.: Defense Manpower Data Center, 2000.

Wright, Jerome, "Adding to Police Ranks Rankles," *Memphis Commercial Appeal*, February 1, 2009. As of November 11, 2009:
http://www.commercialappeal.com/news/2009/feb/01/adding-to-ranks-rankles/

Zhao, Jihong, Nicholas P. Lovrich, and Quint Thurman, "The Status of Community Policing in American Cities: Facilitators and Impediments Revised," *Policing: An International Journal of Police Strategies & Management*, Vol. 22, No. 1, 1999, pp. 74–92.

Personnel management is a critical but oft neglected function of police organizations. While much attention is given to recruiting and retention, these are only tools for accomplishing a larger goal: achieving and maintaining the profile of officers by experience and rank that satisfies agency needs and officer career aspirations. Police agencies often have little ability to assess their organization and environment, and they receive little guidance on how best to build and maintain their workforces. In this monograph, the authors seek to fill the gap of information available to police agencies through a survey on their recruitment and retention practices. The survey, sent to every U.S. police agency with at least 300 sworn officers, sought to document such characteristics as authorized and actual strength by rank, officer work and qualifications, compensation, and recruiting efforts. The authors used these data to provide an overview of current recruitment and retention practices, to describe how they affected police recruitment and personnel profiles, and to identify future research needs. Findings include that police compensation, city size, and crime rates had statistically significant effects on police recruiting. Advertising and recruiting incentives had little effect on the number of recruits. Cohort sizes and structures highlighted current and future personnel management challenges. To facilitate comparative and longitudinal analyses of police staffing, the authors recommend ongoing national data collection.

OBJECTIVE ANALYSIS.
EFFECTIVE SOLUTIONS.

$22.00

RAND publications are available at www.rand.org

This product is part of the RAND Corporation monograph series. RAND monographs present major research findings that address the challenges facing the public and private sectors. All RAND monographs undergo rigorous peer review to ensure high standards for research quality and objectivity.

ISBN 978-0-8330-5068-7

52200

9 780833 050687

MG-960-NIJ

freedom from depression

6 keys to eliminating emotional pain

Best Seller
INTERNATIONAL

PQW713074

by:
anthony piparo, ph.d.